FOUL BOTTOMS

JOHN QUIRK

ADLARD COLES NAUTICAL
LONDON

To all the wonderful members of my family.

...particularly the ones who are still speaking to me.

Published by Adlard Coles Nautical
an imprint of A & C Black Publishers Ltd
36 Soho Square, London W1D 3QY
www.adlardcoles.com

Copyright © J Quirk 2010

First edition 2010

ISBN 978-1-4081-2269-3

A CIP catalogue record for this book is available from the British
Library.

This book is produced using paper that is made from wood grown in
managed, sustainable forests. It is natural, renewable and recyclable.
The logging and manufacturing processes conform to the
environmental regulations of the country of origin.

Typeset in ITC Legacy 9.5pt on 12pt
Printed and bound in Spain by GraphyCems

CONTENTS

FIRST LOVE

Boats are like girls. You never forget your first

First boats can be like first loves. Their attractions and faults tend to be magnified over the years. Even the most broken down old clunker can be remembered as a classic beauty when seen through the golden glow of memory. (I'm talking about boats here.)

My first boat was a dainty classic, an 8 foot clinker stem dinghy which was acquired for two and a half weeks pre-tax wages. Ten quid was a lot of money to a teenager then. Every plank and rib was intact, the varnish had all but disappeared, she wore a piece of black rubber hose as a fender and her bottom had been daubed with tar. To me, she was as beautiful as *Dyarchy*... It cost a further £1.50 and 24 hours for British Railways to collect it from a sniffy South Coast yacht club, steal the beautifully spliced painters and dump it on the platform of our grimy local station.

Two stalwart mates were pressed to help me hernia it the last few miles to the shed where she was to be restored. The hill at the end of our street, which had been such a delight in our tobogganing and soap box days, now stood in front of us as though it were the South Col seen from an Everest base camp. As we were sprawled in the street, trying to summon the strength to draw a dying breath, another mate pulled up to show off his new car. Well, it was new to him, but it had rattled out of the factory in the late '20s on cobweb wire wheels with just enough power to drive a small sewing machine. A few comments were pointedly thrown at the driver to this effect. And it had the desired result. 'She's got plenty of power. Here, throw that thing on the roof and I'll show you.' We found the strength to heave it aboard the tiny car. It fitted as snugly as Norman Wisdom's cap. 'You two will have to stand on the running boards and hold it on,' directed the driver. I was to sit astride the bonnet and secure the stem. The freeboard was reduced considerably as the car snuggled down on its suspension, groaning under the load of four passengers, one

dinghy and general old age. The driver stuck his head out of the window, looked behind him and suddenly reversed across the street and up the hill. We were a bit surprised at this direction, but the lowest gear in cars then was reverse and our driver needed the lowest one he could find. Boiling like your Granny's kettle, the whole crazy convoy ground its way painfully up the hill with a screaming engine, clouds of steam and the strong smell of barbecued clutch. And I do mean painfully. I was straddled over the radiator, gripping the sides of the bonnet like a rodeo rider. The car's mascot was the only thing preventing me from sliding overboard, and the fact that it was branding itself into my hide only added to the cowboy analogy. We arrived in triumph, the car heralding our arrival by blowing its top radiator hose. Ouch. The memory of it still brings tears to my eyes.

Over the next few weeks, the dinghy was blowtorched and scraped down to bare wood, sanded to death and lovingly re-varnished. She had light-coloured planking and contrasting darker transom, stem and wale strake. She also had the most beautifully swept bottom boards following the curve of the bilge. I found out why a previous owner had embalmed her bottom in tar; she had spent too many years drying out on sandy beaches, grains of which had become trapped between the planks and she never fully took up. Although she carried four passengers comfortably, and was the sweetest rowing dink I can remember, it was quite beyond my skills to keep up with her leaks. Eventually, she was unloaded at a profit and I bought a chubby plastic hull that I dressed up with mahogany trim. It rowed like a wet loaf.

Many of us may have had the opportunity to catch up with old boats and old loves. I don't quite know how to put this, but it strikes me that although both may have increased their displacement over the years due to water retention, at least the old boats still conform to their original dimensions... I would welcome my first boat back in a heartbeat, but the first love...? Let me get back to you on that.

MOOR, is MORE

Arthur learns the hard way. Too much can sometimes be more than enough

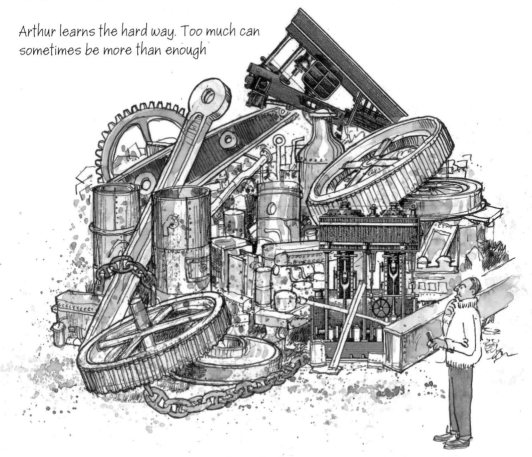

They say that many self-made men worship their creator. Not so with Arthur. He was all his own work and on the whole, he had not made a bad job of it. From dirt-poor backstreet beginnings, he had bludgeoned and swashbuckled his way to the A-list of Black Country society. He was, at middle age, a Birmingham nut-and-bolt baron. He had the eye and the taste for some of the finer things of life, and had the funds – often in cash – to purchase the odd whim without wincing.

Captivated by a shapely bottom lying in the sun on the beach of a Welsh estuary, Arthur saw the 'For Sale' sign and acquired his first boat, a sweet lined pre-war cruising sloop. He couldn't help himself and beat the vendor down just for the hell of it. He passed over a furtive bundle of assorted company cheques and used fivers seasoned with machine oil and mothballs and handed similar packages to the local boat yard to put his new passion through the equivalent of the 'Intensive Care' Section at Max Factor. She was a gleaming vision of perfection as she slid back into the water and towed to a boatyard mooring.

'What do you use at the bottom of those mooring chains?' he demanded of the yard manager. When shown a sample of the odd engine fly wheel and an assortment of concrete blocks, Arthur sniffed. 'That's not a mooring. I'll bring you a mooring.'

Back at his Works, he scoured the yard for lumps of metal that were too heavy for the staff to steal and he had not been able to sell. He assembled a metal mountain of old seized truck

engines, half a dozen factory cog wheels and random leftovers from the industrial revolution. This was craned onto his biggest lorry and crocheted together with loops of chain that was too heavy for the *Titanic*...

History does not record how the boat yard actually laid Arthur's mooring but locals still say that it was the biggest load of metal voluntarily sent to the bottom since the Germans scuppered their North Sea fleet at Scarpa Flow. He was chuffed to have the heaviest mooring on the Welsh coast. 'After all,' he said, handing some strange smelling notes across the bar that evening, 'you can't take chances with a 25 footer'.

History also does not record Arthur's exact reaction when his wife told him she thought he needed a little help for their first weekend afloat and had invited her nephew along. His blood pressure edged into the purple zone. 'What do you want to drag that idiot along for?'

'He's not an idiot, he's at university,' she countered.

'All that brain and no intelligence. He will probably wind up at some Looney council dreaming up titles for useless new jobs,' reflecting on how his own hard upbringing compared with that of this pampered spoilt to death streak of bone and pimples.

The student eventually came to understand Arthur's barked commands and scurried from port to starboard when tacking with the speed of cold treacle. Initially, each bellow of 'Lee Ho!' caused the student to gawp around for an unseen crew member called Leo who the skipper might be addressing.

They returned from their shakedown day trip and picked up the mooring. That mooring. Arthur was flushed with a mixture of pride, sun-seared elation and brown ale, tinged with regret that National Service had been abolished.

He fussed around with his new love before rowing his crew ashore for dinner at a hotel and to give his expense account the work-out it deserved. It was pitch black and the tide was just on the ebb as they rowed back. 'Funny, I can't seem to see her,' said Arthur, squinting through a slight sea mist and fog of alcohol. 'She couldn't have drifted. Not on that mooring she couldn't!'

'And she wouldn't have swung around too much, Uncle,' squeaked a falsetto behind his ear. 'There was lots of loose chain, so I tightened it all up for you.'

As the tide rose, Arthur's new love could not rise with it. She was pulled down onto her mooring. That mooring. It poked its iron fingers through every plank and frame of her lovely hull. Arthur tried to look at the whole business as a win-win situation. The insurance agent made a few bob for himself when he sold the wreck to Arthur for a handful of strange smelling banknotes. So did Arthur when he salvaged: the lead keel, some of the rigging, the Stuart Turner which he used as a generator in his next boat, a few tools, a pewter beer mug, two emergency bottles of scotch and a pair of Wellingtons.

There was one other winner. It is not often that a bored Army recruiting officer gets a university-trained volunteer standing on the doorstep waiting for him to open, asking how soon he can join up and what are the chances of an overseas posting. And nobody before had ever said Yemen looked attractive...

The Swinging Sixties

A relic of the short back and sides era himself, Quirkie ponders life in the slower lane

Life was different in the early sixties. Back in the days when I carried a comb and you could put your nationality as English on a UK census form without the threat of being fined or jailed, there was no need for speed limits on inland waterways and you could take your mother to see a John Wayne western without it resulting in a life time of therapy. We strolled out of the cinema, still arguing about who shot Liberty Vallance and found a slight problem with the car. It had undergone a tune-up by experts that day and had been reassembled minus a few critical washers. It had leaked enough petrol to set fire to Kuwait.

Two young blokes in the next car saw our problem and offered us a lift home (this is the early sixties, remember.) On being invited in for the obligatory cup of tea, they remarked on the boat pictures on the wall, between squadrons of flying ducks (sixties), and said they had just returned from a holiday on the Norfolk Broads.

'Four of us hired this sailing cruiser,' said the taller one. 'It had no engine, so we had the right of way over all motor boats, but not many of them seemed to know that. By the end of

the week, we had developed a bit of an attitude towards those motor boats – particularly hire boats – which would not give way and tooted at us as if they were in a traffic jam in Chiswick High Street.

'On our last night, the four of us were rowing back from the pub in the dinghy with one white knuckle of freeboard, when out of the darkness we heard a strange noise. Around the bend came one of these newfangled plastic speedboats with a big American outboard. Must have been 25 hp (sixties, remember). There were two people in it, they roared past us, throwing a wash like a tsunami and there was nothing we could do. The water slopped over the gunwale and we sank by inches. First, the best brogues, grey flannels and then the Harris Tweed jackets (very sixties). Then we were swimming.

'This was the last straw. Bloody motor boats! We swam back to our boat, bailed the dinghy and two of us got into dry clothes and set off river after the speedboat. We rowed forever. We rowed till our hands burned and our backs ached. We rowed so far that we rowed ourselves sober. We were just realising what a stupid exercise this was when we saw a white plastic speedboat tied up alongside a motor cruiser. Probably one of those who would not give way to us. A quick whispered plan of action, we brought the dinghy alongside and 'Tally Ho, chaps! Over the top!' (We were all very conscious at the time that we had won the War only a few years before.)

Very carefully, we eased over the transom. There were two blokes asleep in the cabin. Fuelled by anger, elation, pure adrenaline and about four pints of Worthington 'E', I'm sure we had them out of the cabin and over the side before they woke up. I remember a flurry of deck chair striped pyjamas; the other one was in Paisley (sixties). As the second one hit the drink I remember wondering if they could swim. They could. And they could shout and curse us at the same time. We were in the dinghy and just heading back downstream when we heard this familiar sound. Around a bend came this white plastic speedboat. It appeared possible, just possible, that we may have picked the wrong boat...'

JACK'S JETTY

Quirkie and a batch of school chums help a
neighbour to rebuild a jetty and learn one
of the basic Commandments of boating

Jack used to reckon that seagoing types had it dead easy. The tide comes in. Then it goes out. They even have little printed tables that tell the sea when, and how high, to come in. But not so for those intrepid mariners who keep their boats on inland waterways. Particularly the Severn. A slight thawing of the slush in Wales and it thinks it is the Chagres River in Panama that was said to rise 170 feet while you are having a cup of tea.

Jack was our enigmatic neighbour who ran the local cinema and used to let us into matinees free to educate us on classic films. He and his family also introduced us to the joys of messing about in boats. They kept a neat 22 foot motor cruiser on the Severn at an idyllic landing stage of chocolate box cuteness, flanked by the obligatory weeping willows. One frigid spring, after a particularly exuberant display of Chagres Syndrome, the flood subsided and the jetty was gone.

Quick! How do you replace this in a hurry, at limited expense, of course? No problem. Jack knew all about major constructions over rivers. His cinema had just shown the trailer for *The Bridge On The River Kwai*. He also had an army of pimply schoolboy volunteers, itching to help. We proudly called ourselves 'The Bluebottle Brigade' after our Goon Show hero. We called everybody 'Captinj' and saluted a lot.

Jack outlined the plan of action to the assembled Brigade: a series of metal posts would be driven into the riverbed, 'here, here and here', the framework and timber deck would be bolted on top. 'Any questions, chaps?'

We listed the materials required and the next Saturday we Steptoed the neighbourhood. The local scrap metal dealer, the council tip and an unguarded demolition site yielded enough building material to crush the life out of the home-made roof rack on Jack's polished to death 1948 Riley.

The next morning was the coldest I can remember. The grass was white and brittle with frost. The river was still high and crazy paved with slabs of ice sliding seawards at walking pace. Jack was the only one old enough to own a pair of long trousers, and our knots-in-cotton knees shivered together like wind chimes. 'Now, be careful,' warned Jack for the tenth time that

morning and every two minutes afterwards, as the budding Baden-Powells swarmed over the precarious structure growing out from the bank. By mid-afternoon we had reached where the river was six foot deep, and it was done. Alec Guinness would have been proud of us. Jack certainly was.

With further 'be carefuls' ringing in our ears, we began to pick up the tools.

A word of advice to those painting boats, gutters and working on jetties: don't stand back to admire your work.

There was a gasp, a windmilling of arms and an almighty crackle and splash. Jack spluttered up though the icy paving of river ice and grabbed a handful of down stream willow. Helped by bits of branches and fencing wire and lots of 'be careful's, we dragged him into the shallows. By the time we hauled him through the mud and up the bank, he looked like the *Creature from the Grey Lagoon.*

The only place to clean him up was an ice crusted cattle trough at the top of the meadow. Jacks teeth were chattering like a flamenco dancer's castanets and he seemed to have frozen his grey cells as well.

'Humphrey...' he shivered, 'Get Humphrey...' One of the brighter members of the Bluebottle Brigade made the connection. Jack, the ultimate film buff, was a fan of Humphrey Bogart. In the boot of the car he had spotted a rancid dog haired trench coat. Just the thing Humphrey would wear against the studio fog in the last reel of Casablanca.

Today, the idea of a man naked beneath an old trench coat, driving a carload of schoolboys, would raise eyebrows, headlines and maybe questions in the House. In those innocent days, we had not heard of hypothermia nor heaters in cars, and when we arrived at Jack's home we failed to pick up on the comment from Jack's wife.

We heaved him out from behind the wheel and up to his front door with the urgency of getting Shackleton to the whaling station on South Georgia. Two of us supported his elbows as Mrs Jack opened the door. He was recovering the power of speech and started to mumble in pidgin novocaine, the dialect of the dentist chair.

'Um a bid code, Luv. Ne'er bin thus code before...' A shivering spasm shook the front of Humphrey open to the winter air.

She lowered her gaze and grinned, 'yes...I can see that...'

YOU'RE ALRIGHT, JACK

Quirkie gets afloat and discovers the joy of messing about in boats, courtesy of an enigmatic neighbour

We youngsters who lived in that industrial brick and pebble dash Midland suburb fancied we were a cut above our other school friends. Our neighbour Jack had a series of boats on the river and it was unthinkable for him, his wife and young daughter to drive down there unless the car was jammed to capacity with appreciative youngsters. In those pre-seatbelt days, it was quite normal that most young passengers had another one on their lap.

The first boat was a 22 foot Blackwater built cruiser with an 8 hp Stuart Turner, in which the navigable lengths of the Severn and Avon were explored. The owners slept aboard, the rest of us were thrilled to pitch a tent on the riverbank. We caught fish, cooked and ate them, just as we had seen our celluloid heroes do. If anyone wants to recreate the unique flavour and texture of Severn chub, boil up a batch of cardboard boxes with some old socks, add a dashing handful of fuse wire clippings to replicate the bones. Season to taste.

Jack felt that a larger boat was called for and scoured the tiny black and white pictures in the back of *Motor Boat and Yachting* which, apart from the *Exchange and Mart*, was about the only option in those days. On neither the Severn nor Avon, was there anything appealing in his limited price range. A converted pinnace on the Thames looked good in the photo... but not when we climbed aboard. On our disappointed return journey we called in every Thames boatyard and scoured the 'For Sale' notices. Under a pile of old tarps with a few bilge strakes missing we found *Ryegate*, an affordable 30 foot centre wheel house cruiser 'needing work', as they say. We teenage

enthusiasts in the back seat assured Jack that with our combined talents (limited) and enthusiasm (boundless) we could have her ship shape and Bristol fashion in no time.

She was trucked to Gloucester docks, hoisted into the basin by a steam crane now serving as a museum piece. We bilge pumped our way with an overheating engine up to Worcester where the refit began. It is probably indicative of how our society has changed that in one winter she was transformed by a team of willing teenagers and their families. 'Mr J, my dad has some mahogany he has been saving from before the War, enough he says to make you some new wheelhouse windows.'

We learned to use Scarsten scrapers by the boxload, and had the paint work and mahogany brightwork gleaming. I recall adding a T&G mahogany bulkhead which still looked good 50 years later. All this was done while afloat, without power tools of course, and only the most basic borrowed hand tools.

Through the next few summers at weekends, *Ryegate* – laden with her enthusiastic crew of young helpers – cruised the length of the river in perpetual party mood. We swam from May till October in those golden days of youth. We would lie on the decks in the evenings, holding fishing rods, listening to the wood pigeons in utter silence, just wanting to hold onto the memory of those soft summer twilights before we had to return to our jobs and night school courses in the brick-lined city. In warm weather, we would jump into somebody's car after work, drive down and use the boat as a swimming platform. The river felt as warm as brown Windsor soup. I remember someone saying what a pity it was that the river finished at Gloucester. I thought how wonderful it is that with a slight detour from the river through the Berkley Ship Canal, you can get to any seawater part of the globe you wanted.

After the Heart of England Rivers had been retraced, our thoughts were set on going to sea down the Bristol Channel. The first trip was almost enough for Jack to consider having *Ryegate* shipped back by road. With only one week of precious holiday each, we considered the weather forecast to be 'good enough' and headed out into a rising wind against tide that tested ship and crew. One wave crest gave *Ryegate* an uppercut that broke the anchor out of its lashings on the fore deck and tossed it into the mast. The scar is still there.

But the ensuing days of fair weather and gentle seas had us all captivated at the joys of coastal cruising. While on a visit to Cornwall, Jack found a small yard that could build a husky new motor cruiser for little more than *Ryegate* was worth after her refit (or so he told us and his wife). A lucky and swift sale of *Ryegate* allowed the new boat, *Spring Maid*, to be built over the winter.

By this time, some of us kids had grown up and some even had cars. There was comparatively little to do with a new boat and a new diesel, except keep up with the paint and varnish and enjoy it.

And we did. *Spring Maid* was kept on the Hamble where each summer we explored the South Coast and Channel Islands. Jack had taken his family there for summer holidays for the previous six years and each morning and evening he would drag them round St Peter Port harbour admiring the boats and envying those aboard. His happiest times were spent enjoying the first cup of tea of the day in his blue and white mug, wearing matching pyjamas, sitting in the cockpit and chatting with admiring onlookers.

Each winter, we cruised back to Cornwall to take advantage of the cheaper winter lay-up costs and convivial company at the boat yard. Eventually, most of his volunteer crew grew up, paired off, took on responsibilities and started putting deposits on semis.

To escape this epidemic of growing up syndrome, I took a job in Africa and flew out with a copy of H Rider Haggard's classic in my 22 kilos of luggage. At weekends, I planned to be an explorer. With memories of seeing how dashing Steward Granger looked in the 1950 film, and Haggard's book as a guide, I hoped to find the back way in to *King Solomon's Mines*. However, it did not quite work out that way. I found myself building game viewing lodges, and enjoyed adventures I had previously only seen from the 1/9ds in Jack's cinema.

Now he was often single handed, Jack sold *Spring Maid* for a smaller fibreglass boat that could be heaved around on a trailer. One summer he based this boat in Watermouth Bay on the Southern shore of the Bristol Channel and offered her for use by the old crew members. This coincided with my being in UK on leave and after the sudden sunsets of the tropics, it was a delight to experience the long languid summer evenings from a small boat nudging into all those snug little harbours and anchorages during what must have been the calmest and sunniest June on record.

The old crew members have stayed in touch for over 40 years. Some of them get together and charter boats to rekindle those magic days of youth, and step off them knowing that they no longer face a winter of battered knuckles, too frozen to bleed, and Scarsten scrapers.

By the merest chance, many years later I met *Ryegate*'s current owners and have since enjoyed three memorable holidays aboard with them. That is another story, but what a delightful discovery that was, snugged up in my old berth with its little reading light, in the cool stillness of a spring evening, listening to a later generation of wood pigeons. Nostalgia is every bit as good as you hoped it would be.

So all thanks to you Jack... you're alright.

RICHER THAN ALL HIS TRIBE

A wealthy new boating neighbour with the same shoe size moves into the end of Quirkie's street

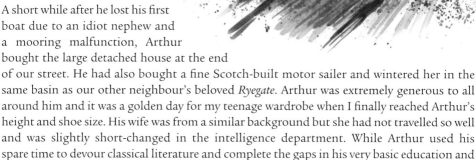

A short while after he lost his first boat due to an idiot nephew and a mooring malfunction, Arthur bought the large detached house at the end of our street. He had also bought a fine Scotch-built motor sailer and wintered her in the same basin as our other neighbour's beloved *Ryegate*. Arthur was extremely generous to all around him and it was a golden day for my teenage wardrobe when I finally reached Arthur's height and shoe size. His wife was from a similar background but she had not travelled so well and was slightly short-changed in the intelligence department. While Arthur used his spare time to devour classical literature and complete the gaps in his very basic education and was happy to share the rewards of his hard work, to his wife these rewards were to be protected and polished.

Few visitors were ever admitted across the gleaming threshold of the vast house in which the two of them lived. No cooking smells ever took refuge in the flock wallpaper; all entertaining was done in fine restaurants, as otherwise Arthur would come home at night to a hearty couple of tomatoes on a lettuce leaf with a slice of off-the-shelf pork pie...

He would stride past us at weekends on his way to his boat, with a cheery wave, exercising the big ends of his Jaguar, leaving Ford Pops and lesser traffic rocking in a slipstream of Castrol R, medium rare Michelins and expensive cigar smoke. As he had the facilities, every deck fitting aboard was removed and chromed till the boat twinkled like Harry Winston's shop window. In the summer it was moored ahead of Jack's boat. In the winter, it hibernated beneath tailored cream covers while *Ryegate* huddled beneath a patched set of army surplus canvases with the flexibility of three ply and a smell that the effluence from the local industrial estate could not diminish.

As the rain became warmer, announcing an English spring, van loads of specialists from The Works lemminged over every inch of Arthur's boat putting her through the equivalent of the Max Factor intensive care service.

Jack had rebuilt his 30 foot centre wheel house *Gibbs* over three winters assisted by an inexhaustible stream of teenage neighbours and friends. His ability to Pied Piper this team of willing helpers caused the locals to refer to *Ryegate*'s winter berth as Hamlin Hard.

Arthur was a prominent member of the local yacht club and he would generously invite a load of us to dinners as his guests. I think this was to enjoy some lively company that was denied him in his own home. The evening he was made Commodore, we were there in borrowed blazers, while Arthur had a magnificent new rig from Gieves. His wife had asked him to bring aboard the box of wine and a bag of clean clothes ('I have told you not to leave any clothes aboard, dear, they will smell of boat') from the car before it got dark. Then his house/boat-proud wife noticed an unforgivable sin aboard... There was a smudged fingermark on the aft mooring cleat, which was otherwise, like the rest of the boat, in the state of flawless

perfection. She got out the metal polish and had to move this silly bit of rope so that she could clean it properly. Arthur returned, fully Gieves-rigged in a blazer that cost more than my car, with an armload of boxes, put one foot on the boat from the jetty… and – showing how little effort it takes to move 12 tons of boat – pushed the unsecured stern of the boat out…

Arthur was inaugurated, flanked by club members ablaze with blazers and buttons, in Jack's boat-flavoured Navy surplus sweater and a pair of my jeans.

When Jack and Arthur decided to take their boats via the Sharpness canal to the Bristol Channel it created a frenzy of winter activity aboard both boats. Arthur commanded a set of sheer legs be made for drying out in tidal harbours. We whittled a pair out of two 6 inch square bulks of timber reclaimed from a demolished house. Acne-covered young engineering and electrical students spent their weekends writhing in *Ryegate*'s bilges among the paint thickened wiring with oil, gaskets, filters and plasters, changing hoses and pipes and fussing over the old Graymarine side valve engine so that it would rattle and smoke as reliably in the Channel as it did on the river. Arthur addressed the problem by simply ordering a new diesel engine to be sent down from The Works with a team of mechanics and the firm's catering van. He supervised the operation with smoked salmon sandwich in one hand and brown ale in the other.

Jack's young daughter passed him a mug of tea and a cheese sandwich through a vacant plank which we were replacing as he came up for air. He was degreasing the bilge beneath the engine while Arthur conducted his engine transplant in a spotless white sweater that would have cost more than the materials for *Ryegate*'s refit. 'I think Uncle Arthur (all unrelated adults were called either uncle or auntie in those days) must be the richest man in the whole world,' said the child. Jack's comments were not recorded.

Arthur was always out onto the river well ahead of us where he sat on his mooring. He had subscriptions to every boating magazine printed in English, which he skimmed through with the attention you normally give to reading a bus ticket. Then he passed them on to Jack... who passed them on to the rest of us.

Occasionally we would see Arthur leave his mooring and proceed down river to a riverside pub. He would call ahead to ensure that his mooring lines would be taken and his expense account would be welcome. He either had somebody from his wife's family aboard or a business connection he needed to soften up.

Both skippers had chosen a June assault on the channel and they arrived outside the sea lock at Sharpness at the same time. Tingling with excitement, the crew of *Ryegate* prepared for a 4am departure. Arthur said he might leave it a tide or two. He was not too keen on getting up for these dawn patrols.

Ryegate's crew, full of anticipation, seasickness tablets and a touch of terror, left in the dark at an hour before high water the next morning. For all those aboard, and particularly the owner, Jack, this maiden sea cruise was the culmination of a lot of fireside planning and hard work. Despite our ignorance, incompetence and near-death experiences, it was a brilliant adventure. We were captivated. All of us have since enjoyed a life-long association with the sea.

Arthur and his immaculate motor yacht with the brand new diesel engine never left the river. He motored back to his mooring; those new sheer legs remained in the same immaculate, meticulously cleaned condition as the rest of his boat. Here was a man who had everything, except perhaps two little items: companionship and happiness...

Fast forward 30 years and I was in the UK for Jack's funeral. He had actually collapsed and died aboard his boat as he was fitting out for a cruise to Cornwall. Although we had all grown up and moved away, Jack still had enthusiastic helpers, in a son-in-law and two grand-daughters, his daughter having married one of the original fitting out crew. After the funeral, she and I drove an aged and widowed Arthur to one of his favourite riverside pubs. This was the posh one, the one that did not serve chips in the dining room.

'I used to envy your father,' he said to her over lunch and as much brown ale as a 76 year old non-designated driver could comfortably hold. 'I never knew the colour of your waterline; your boat was always so loaded down with a crowd of you having a good time. And then you went off to sea and saw all those places I hoped I would see in my boat. Apart from a few in-laws who wanted a free feed, I had nobody who was interested in coming out with me. I entertained a few business people and Lodge members, but that was about it. I overheard someone making a comment about me at the Club once. They said I was either with clueless or crewless. Ada came from a rough background, not her fault she was a bit out of her depth with some of these hoity toity types. She left school at 14 your know. She was a good wife to me for fifty years.' When she became ill, Arthur gave up his boat and nursed her for the last five years of her life.

This hard-edged businessman, who used to snack on other industrialists for morning tea, wiped an eye before continuing. 'I have met a few wealthy people in my life, love, but your father was the richest man I ever knew'.

THE PERFECTIONIST

Every weekend he had all the gear out of his 45 footer, and checked everything in preparation for a voyage down the Bristol Channel. Just one small point...

We passed his mooring every weekend that summer. The gleaming 45 foot twin screw motor cruiser was kept outside a fine period house with extensive lawns sloping down to the river. Every weekend, these lawns were littered with the contents of the boat. Mattresses were out to air, ropes hanked into tangled coils, ladders, tool boxes and dozens of paint tins stood in a chaotic jumble along the jetty as the owner systematically brought the entire contents of the boat ashore, fussed about with them, then at the end of the day, put them all back again. You would not believe a 45 foot could hold so much gear.

'I don't think Eisenhower took that much stuff with him on D Day,' remarked Jack. 'It looks like stocktaking day in Portsmouth Dockyard.'

'He's planning to take her down the Bristol Channel next month,' explained Arthur as we took his mooring lines in one Sunday evening. 'Of course, he only bought it at the end of last year. Then he had the whole boat refitted in the Basin this winter. All painted, full electrical and mechanical overhaul. Cost him a fortune. Can't see what's left for him to do.'

The following weekend saw the same litter of equipment across the lawn. When the owner was not toothbrushing between the bottom boards of the lovely varnished dinghy, he diligently wet and dried the inside of a brass megaphone before giving it another careful coat of red paint. Then he polished the outside until it shone like a guardsman's helmet. Clearly, here was a man who was prepared for anything the Bristol Channel could throw at him.

Looking back on those primitive days of the early sixties, the Bristol Channel was talked about in hushed reverence like those old charts which proclaim 'Here be Dragons...' It was considered on the river to be the Cape Horn of boating achievements. You could not take it on in anything less than a 45 foot twin-engined real sea boat, they said. There were tales of near death experiences, swept away dinghies, smashed superstructures and sheer blind terror. To have made the passage from Sharpness to say, Ilfracombe and back was the mark of a true seaman. Very few reported having an enjoyable experience doing it.

The next time we passed the mooring of the perfectionist owner, the lawns were recovering from looking like a circus site and there was no sign of the boat. 'So how did our mate go down the Channel?' we asked Arthur who knew everything there was to know about the river. And everything else. 'Interesting. He got down to Sharpness with a hired crewman who knew the Channel. They were about to open the sea lock when he makes a discovery. You know he took everything out of the boat to check it and put it back? Well, he forgot the charts. Instead of locking back in and sending for them, he puts the crew bloke ashore, tells him to get a taxi, go back and collect the charts off the mantelpiece and he will hang around outside the lock, in the Channel and wait for him. Silly bugger. Of course, I could have told him he could not stem the ebb and hang about when it got going and you have to leave on high water anyway. And that's what happened, the tide started to take him down channel; it runs about 8 knots there, you know. Somehow he made it down to Portishead without hitting anything. He should have pulled in there but no, he was determined to push on. He had memorised the leading lights to one of the harbours. It was getting dark and he planned to keep going until he saw the lights and follow them in.

'And he did. By a miracle, he made it to his memorised harbour. But it was August Bank Holiday, wasn't it? Fairground on the quay and the place was blazing like bloody Blackpool. Looking for leading lights would be like trying to pick a star in the Milky Way. He hung around till after midnight, waiting for the fair to shut down and put the lights out. He almost made it. Ran aground on a beach outside the harbour and he was lucky he managed to stay afloat and get inside the next morning.

'The boat is still down there. You can't miss it. It has a big 'For sale' sign on it.'

Fortunately, he had memorised the leading lights

Storm and a D Cup

The ever-generous Arthur sets Quirkie up with a memorable cross-Channel passage

It's not often you get this lucky.

A friend of Arthur's was the proud owner of a new thirty something foot GRP motor sailer based on the South Coast. After some coastal cruising, he had sailed her over to the Continent with his wife and a younger crew member. Arthur filled me in on this when he appeared on our doorstep one summer evening. 'Bit of a choppy passage,' he said. 'Slight mutiny. Wife and crew now don't do Channel crossings. Told him to find someone else to bring it back; they'll see him at home. Of course, I would love to go over and give him a hand but I can't get away at the moment. Got a Lodge meeting Saturday night. I owe him a favour for a deal we once did.' He paused to look over his shoulder just in case someone from Inland Revenue was within listening distance. 'Jack said you were crewing for him this long weekend and thought you would jump at his chance.' He handed over an envelope. 'Here is an airline ticket. There's a bit of Walking around Money there too. I will run you to the airport after lunch on Friday. Harry, the skipper, will meet you at the airport at the other end. Little fat bugger with a moustache. When you see his wife, don't mention the face lift... You bring the boat back Saturday. Catch the train back here Sunday afternoon.'

Why do I suspect that Arthur didn't often hear the word 'no'? Maybe because nobody could get a word in when he is in full flight.

The ever generous industrialist passed over an envelope containing a one-way airline ticket comfortably upholstered with bank notes. Some of them smelt a bit strange... It turned out to be nearly a week's wages at the time.

I joined the smart centre cockpit craft for a day with the original crew, to get acquainted with how the owner liked to

Meanwhile, on the way to the airport with Arthur...

While we are back in the swinging sixties, consider how different motoring was then. Not just on 6p a litre, but there were no speed limits on the open roads, no motorways to speak of, no seat belts, no MOT nor random breath tests. People could manage whole sentences without the 'F word', there was neither airport security nor PC police. Here is a typical journey of the time.

It's lucky I'm still here...

Arthur was late. Very late. He scooped me up from the kerb as if he were a getaway driver for *Bonnie and Clyde*. The leather lined Jag was filled with cigar smoke and more brandy fumes than our Christmas pudding, and his breath would have set fire to litmus paper. It was the first time I had ever done 100 mph in a car and I still recall some of Arthur's non-stop 3000 rpm post-lunch diction as he blasted through the traffic with one hand on the wheel, chomping on a cigar and dispensing comment, opinion and rude signals with the other. This conversation was delivered in less than two miles of Friday afternoon traffic on a busy dual carriageway...

'Sorry I'm a bit late. Had this lunch with a bloke I used to know. He paid, so you can tell the bugger's after something. Ordered sushi. Ever had it? Don't bother. Just like bloody bait. Not even cooked. Might be alright for feeding Japs, but it would never catch on here. Yes, well, the skipper, Norman, he'll collect you at the other end. He's alright I suppose, but you got to watch these little buggers. They try to make up for being short changed. Napoleon Complex. If a bloke's under 5'8", it increases as the cube of the distance in inches below that. Brains too near their arse. Of course, his wife's got the money, you know. Why else would he marry her? I think you met her at my Lodge Night. Don't mention the face lift. She's loaded, but as tight as a duck's arse. Shopped around and went to the lowest bidder. And it shows. Should have had her snappers fixed first. I'm not kidding; she could eat a Granny Smith through a chicken wire fence. I think she had to have bought him the boat though. He's got nothing. I had to back him on this, er, thing we did. He knows bugger all about boats too, surprised he made it across the Channel. Still, I s'pose France is big enough not to miss. Like to take my boat up to Paris, you know. There's bloody miles of canals over there you know, not little narrowboat stuff like ours, proper seagoing boats can go all the way to the Med. Like to do that one day too. I'm glad I didn't go for automatic one of these, you know, you only get three speeds. This has got four and overdrive. Watch this, that prat in the Zephyr in front thinks he's going to overtake the Mini, see? 80 in third and we are still accelerating. Since I put that new diesel in my boat, it's chalk and cheese, you know. Oh yes, like having disc brakes. I can stop her dead in no length, and with the extra power I can kick her stern port or starboard just by a burst forward or astern. Who was it brought that big bird down to Jack's boat the other week? Dark haired piece with the watermelon necklace? All that meat and no potatoes... Look, 105 mph and we're still ticking over. Likes a drink, does this car, mind you; we've got a pump at the works. They fill this every Friday. One for diesel too, I'd bring it down for the boat in jerry cans but the wife says she can smell it in the boot. I might send the van down. What time's your flight? 25 minutes? Oh, plenty of time. I've seen 120 on this on the Halesowen by pass. Traffic's a bit heavy to show you now. You alright for money? Oh I did, didn't I? Well you can always use a bit more, now where's me wallet, oh here, well, take another fiver, just in case... Christ! Did you see the bloke in the Vauxhall? Oi! Dumbo! You gotta pay attention if you want to play in the fast lane... Bloody halfwit...'

I joined the smart centre cockpit craft for a day with the original crew, to get acquainted with how the owner liked to run things. The owner and wife were Arthur's generation, i.e. twice my age, and the wife and crew's mother were old school friends. The crew was off collecting some last minute stuff and would be back for the last night aboard. Even I could see that the owner's wife had been on the receiving end of a sixties facelift. She had a large head and a high brow. With a startled look and glazed complexion from having a reef tucked into her epidermis, she reminded me of a surprised Victorian chamber pot. All that effort and expense on the face lift and she still had Ken Dodd's old teeth. Maybe that would be phase 2 of the urban renewal programme.

I was not prepared for the bonus points that tottered behind a wall of designer shopping bags that advanced along the quay towards us. 'Hello, I'm part of the crew that mutinied. I've just been shopping.' I hoped she was about my age, but she was light years ahead in sophistication and self-assuredness. She had effortlessly elegant thick dark hair, a strong 'don't mess with me' jawline, great smile and a cultured contralto voice that was as soothing as lying in a bath of warm honey. Readers will see at a glance that Quirkie was out of his depth here.

She began decanting the shopping spoils into the aft cabin then came back into the saloon holding a little black number up in front of her. 'My boyfriend, Piers, is taking me out for dinner when we get back.' She mentioned a London restaurant where most of us would get an estimate before considering a reservation. 'Do you think he will like this?' She was a shapely lass, dressed in a T shirt and jeans that fitted like the fuzz on a peach. The dress she held up had a neckline like the one Anita Ekberg's 40Ds bubbled out of in *La Dolce Vita*. She pulled the dress in tighter to show the intended effect.

'I think Piles...'

'Piers ...'

'Whatever, will be delighted.' *I hope it gives him a heart attack and he dies in agony...*

Having a professional interest in such matters, I asked her a few technical questions about support, rigging, compression structures, tensile strength, structural stability and generally defying gravity.

She patted me on the cheek like you would with a pre-schooler.

'You will find out when you're older,' she smiled.

There was the segregation of a Dickensian workhouse aboard. The ladies enjoyed the spacious aft cabin while the skipper and I were jammed into the fo'c'sle, leaving the saloon free as a cargo hold for the shopping which had to be restowed while the ladies slept. The skipper showed me his pre-voyage checklist, opened the cover to a spotless bilge, ran his finger over it and held it up before my eyes. 'Dust,' he announced. 'You vegetable fibre wooden boat types don't get much of this do you?'

'No, we try to keep our bilges clean.'

'This is a Deep Sea Seal.' He pointed to where the prop shaft disappeared into a rubber moulding. 'Sealed for life. You do not have to keep topping them up with grease like the old ones. So much better.'

So that rubber keeps all the sea out, and all the dust in? Hmmm... Looks like a great idea. Is it expensive? If it is, I must tell Arthur about this. He would have to have one.

The wife and crew member had been dispatched to the airport and the skipper showed me his pre-passage check list. Everything was stowed and all in its correct place. Even the dust.

The weather forecast was reasonable; the North Westerly Force 3 to 4 was due to decrease later. Anyway, more important than that, I had to be back at work on Monday. We set the course and headed out across the Channel. The main and headsail were rigged and we motor sailed for home. This was easy, there was even an auto pilot to avoid the labour of holding a course while we took turns to make coffee and open our snacks. Despite the forecast, the wind increased and the ships motion became a bit, er... nauseous. I suspected something was wrong when, going below, I stepped on the cabin sole and it sank under six inches of water.

'But we can't be sinking!' cried our skipper. 'This is a new boat.' And would you believe it, he grabbed the ship's papers and started fumbling for the warranty... I switched on the electric bilge pump, grabbed a bucket and started bailing from the aft cabin out through the hatch. It made not a blind bit of difference. The water level did not retreat.

We were nearly two hours out, and we were sinking. The ship was turned about and we headed back for our port of departure. The quartering wind helped progress, but not my condition. It was more than bilge water I was heaving through that hatch. I was soaked from truck to toe and shivering with cold and fatigue. Where is the sorcerer's apprentice when you need him? We managed to keep the water below the significant bits of the engine. It kept running and pumping. The skipper called the Harbour Master to get us a berth on the drying grid.

We settled on the grid as the tide dropped, the problem was found and dealt with, and with a late afternoon siesta behind us, the wind dropped as promised and we made an uneventful night passage back to the owner's home marina.

A little red Mini pulled up at the marina and the Other Crew Member (OCM) bounced out to collect her cargo of shopping. But there was one item missing. We have all heard of boats been lost to 'moving' rocks, shipping containers, whales, swordfish (just the one), and Coca Cola bottles being pushed up through the hull by the action of the propeller ... but a push-up bra? The secret structural device to support the Dolce Vita dress had escaped from the back of a drawer like a sock from a drier; it had fallen into those dusty bilges where it wrapped the spinning propshaft in a deadly embrace. There was more wire in that bra than Marconi's first radio. It would not have happened with the old traditional stuffing box but the Deep Sea Seal died the death of a thousand cuts, allowing the English Channel free entry to those dust covered bilges.

Before she drove me to the station, I handed over the shredded ruin of the killer bra and hoped she would be able to get a replacement, and that it wouldn't be, er, a let down for her grand dinner with Piles... OK... whatever.

You will be glad to hear that he did not stay the distance; he was tossed and she married a dashing RAF officer and lived happily ever after. In fact, the OCM has stayed in touch for over 40 years. Whereas the rest of us fell to bits with the passing decades, she has remained snap frozen at an indeterminable age of full flowering womanhood. She is not the only item that has stayed unmoved by time. So, it appears, has Britain's Defence system. The OCM produced an RAF officer of her own and it is interesting to reflect that both her husband and son spent their flying careers in the cockpit of the very same Canberra B16 aircraft, 30 years apart...

Some day, son, all of this will be yours . . .

PANIC AT PORLOCK

A delightful setting for Quirkie and co to learn from their mistakes

You must know Porlock Weir, that delightful little haven scooped out of the shingle on the Somerset coast. Even if you haven't been there, you must know it from countless chocolate boxes, jigsaw puzzles and calendars. It is often featured in British magazines consumed by expatriates in foreign climes. A picture of Porlock Weir in the golden glow of autumn light has made many an expat wipe away a tear of nostalgia and consider moving back there. Then they would remember the weather and the tax levels. Others just think it is better to be a second class citizen in somebody else's country than a third class one in your own, turn the page and ask the bar steward to bring them another drink.

Don't just take my word for it; even the pilot of the Junkers 88 shot down on Porlock Beach in 1940 would come back for holidays. The catering is good too; he said you could get no finer cup of tea in England than the brew served up in Minehead police station, where he was arrested.

Not only is the harbour a set designer's dream, but from the village of Porlock a mile or so away, the road over the moors runs up Porlock Hill which up until the sixties would strike terror into the hearts and transmissions of early motorists. Today it is hardly noticed and old timers reckon they have levelled out its 1 in 4 gradient.

It is also the location of one of the most remarkable lifeboat launches ever made. In the days when 'Occupational',' Health' and 'Safety' were separate words in a dictionary, the 3½ ton Lynmouth lifeboat was hauled by men and horses up Countisbury Hill, to over 1,400 feet and down Porlock Hill to be launched at the Weir in one storm-lashed night in January 1899.

One bright high tide morning in Minehead, Jack suggested to the crew of *Ryegate* a quick trip round to Porlock Weir and a brisk stroll up the hill of motoring nostalgia. The crew had apparently been overserved with local scrumpy the night before and by the time we had

packed away the breakfast things and enjoyed a rare smooth and sunlit passage, we judged we were too late to risk the entry through the withies which marked the channel on a falling tide. The seamanlike thing to do, declared Jack, was to leave the boat anchored in these millpond conditions, dinghy ashore and proceed as planned. We would return before high water and come in on a rising tide.

On Jack's magical mystery tour up The Hill, he entertained us with highlights of pre-War motoring. (Wimps could avoid the Hill by using a toll road.) He showed us a lay-by half way up, which was the site where he unbolted the sidecar on his Velocette motorbike and attempted the rest of the Hill without it. Still no luck, so at the next lay-by he decoked the engine on the side of the road. (People had the skills and carried tools do that in those days.) This time with success! Mind you, the girlfriend *de jour* was not impressed by having to dismount and walk up to meet Jack and his steaming machine at the water outlet at the top. As we lurched to the top in our exhausted state, we were cooled by a deliciously refreshing blast of sea breeze.

Breeze? That means wind! From the crest, we could now see a scale model *Ryegate* below, plunging her nose into the whitecaps like a pollie's snout in the public purse. We felt neither pain nor exhaustion as we ran back to the Harbour. Fuelled by the panic of our own ineptitude and last night's scrumpy, we were back at the shingle foreshore, watching the surf pound in like Bondi Beach. There was no way we could launch the dinghy in these conditions.

We were approached by a distinguished nautical looking gent in a blue Guernsey and sawn off sea boots. This was Arthur Leye, the Harbour Master. He calmly led Jack and I aboard his open 'Sixpenny sicker' launch, warmed up the engine, switched over to TVO (Paraffin) and expertly navigated the channel out to where *Ryegate* seemed to be in her death throes. Arthur tried to bring us up to the stern so we could jump aboard the aft deck, but both boats were plunging so much that it was too dangerous. In an exhibition of effortless seamanship, Arthur brought his launch alongside so they were both pitching in unison. We leapt aboard *Ryegate* and were through the wheel house doors before you could say, 'I'm sorry *Ryegate*, we will never leave you home alone again.'

The Graymarine caught on the first swing, the stockless anchor had really dug in and needed to be motored over to break free, then we were rolling into the narrow channel behind Arthur and into a snug non-drying berth in the Pool.

A few lessons to be learned from all this; not only the stupidity of leaving a boat unattended in such exposed conditions but in our haste to pack away the breakfast things, you do not put HP sauce bottles and marmalade jars in with the skipper's shore-going shirt.

SHORE-GOING ETIQUETTE

When Emily Post wrote, in 1922, *Etiquette in Society, in Business, in Politics and the Home*, she missed out on bits like road rage and when some bastard does not give way to 'starboard' and a load of other stuff

Need to deal with an irritating diner at a restaurant? Let Jack, with the subtlety of a dropped kedge, guide you through the minefield of polite social behaviour that Emily Post forgot to mention. You know the Last Supper, that end of cruise dinner where you take the skipper to the best restaurant that will let you in while wearing what is left of your end of cruise wardrobe...?

We were all in red-faced, sun-seared relaxation mode – yet another cruise completed without serous incident. Well, nothing significant enough to be included in these notes. Four of us plus skipper Jack, reeking of clean socks and Lifebuoy soap had fronted up to a promising hotel, had passed the dress code and were soon in a clubby dining room, studying menus and gazing out at magnificent sea views. The sun was a scarlet orb descending towards the sea. We all waited for it to touch the horizon, almost expecting it to hiss...

Among the other innocent civilians quietly dining and admiring the view, and the nerve of the management to charge those prices for their supermarket wine selection, there was one other large table. This was occupied by maybe eight male diners being loudly addressed by a florid Loud Mouth in a blue blazer and a glowing white collar that threatened his circulation. Now the Black Country dialect is a finely developed one, used for giving precise communications over the gentle murmur of a blast furnace. ('Shall I pour, Rodney?') The LM was trying to hide his with a thick coating of posh and no doubt thought he sounded like Wolfitt delivering his Lear. As he soliloquised at the other diners, he was swilling red wine, hacking at a steak and spraying them with both, together with a loud endless commentary. He was one of these people who constantly laugh during their own long-winded stories signifying to others that this was dammed funny and they had better be laughing as well.

It was hard to figure out the relationship here, who would stick it out at the table unless LM was paying the bill? And this meant he was either a boss or senior relative. Probably a boss. Family would have answered back. We had slept blissfully off watch while enduring a wild pounding ride across the Channel with a diesel engine hammering inches from our ears. We had learned to live with our vessel's rock 'n' roll habits on exposed anchorages while waiting for the tide, but the sound of LM droning on could not be ignored. It totally dominated the room and was so loud we could not hold the Last Supper tradition of reminding the others of incidents of the cruise which they all knew before the embroidery began. Conversation was impossible.

Eventually our skipper walked around to behind LM, who was practising for the *Guinness World Record* for the number of chips on one fork, and stopped speaking in mid splatter. 'Excuse me,' asked Jack politely, 'Someone asked if you could repeat the last sentence.' Not since the nano second after I broke wind in Sunday school has the world known such silence. All the other diners held their breath, as if the gunfight at the OK Corral was scheduled for the floor show.

'*Woi?*' demanded the puzzled LM (Blackcountry for 'Why').

'Well, one of the blokes heaving the garbage cans around the back of the hotel did not quite hear it... But everybody else did.'

The laughter was spontaneous around the room. Even at the LM's table where it could mean unemployment or no more Christmas cards. If LM's complexion had been glowing before, he was now incandescent. Laughter and a mild rippling of applause from the other tables greeted our skipper's return. In the ensuing hush, Jack leaned across the table and said, 'On the count of three, all stare at Loud Mouth and laugh... Three.'

How can you not?

Gazing out at magnificent sea views.

EXPLAIN THIS. . .

Quirkie and the crew meet some real sailors, are presented with a mystery and a further lesson in Jack's etiquette course

It was during one long, drawn out winter that we heard of a slide show and lecture to be given by a couple who had spent the last few years cruising the tropics in an old wooden yacht. (No, not the Hiscocks.) One sleeting week night, Jack and the crew joined a room full of armchair dreamers in a soulless Midland hall during the swinging sixties. They may have swung, but they left their memories on other senses. People may remember the sound of The Beatles and the colours of Carnaby Street glamour but these were the days of the once a week bath night, before air conditioning and mechanical ventilation. We all enjoyed home cooked meals, fried or boiled to death in cramped kitchens in those golden days before the deodorant industry and frequent dry cleaning. The hall windows would have been shut since October and that special sixties flavour was overlaid with a few dozen damp raincoats. Then everybody else lit up and coughed.

A fragile elderly couple were introduced by whoever ran the meeting; a brief summary of their ocean voyages was made for those who had not read the modest book they had written. On reflection, it is interesting that the book was not on sale that evening. The guest speaker thanked us all for coming out on such a foul miserable evening. (Hey, we live here. This is normal.) The lights were dimmed and the slide projector hummed into life. We were soon transfixed by the brilliant sunlit images and the modest narrative of the voyagers. He told of how they had owned their boat for many years and cruised in her every summer. While in the West Country one autumn, they both agreed that the prospect of retirement and British winters and gas bills held little appeal, so they just kept on sailing to follow the sun. First it was to Spain and the Med. Then they began crossing oceans and exploring foreign lands, all of which blazed at us from the screen bathed in tropical sunlight... Then the narrator switched the slide projector off, called for the house lights and faced the audience. 'I am afraid that what I am about to tell you does not appear in the book.' He told the room. 'The publishers advised against it, but you can make up your own minds.'

Nearing the end of an ocean crossing and looking for a landfall, he had not been able to get a sun or star sight for several days. The erratic currents made dead reckoning unreliable and they did not know their position within a hundred miles. They were aiming for a friendly little port of entry they had visited two years before which was protected by an offshore reef on which there was a conspicuous light. The weather was foul, with poor visibility. Then his wife went down with stomach pains. *The Ship Captain's Medical Guide* pointed towards appendicitis. He vividly explained his state of mind at the time and his feeling of guilt at placing his wife in this life threatening position.

'The weather was now a real problem. Very high winds and rain squalls which blotted out all visibility. My wife was bravely holding on down below, unable to come on deck. I had been on watch for several days now and was becoming exhausted. Then suddenly, dead ahead and up quite high, was the signal from the light tower of the reef which guarded the harbour. I

only saw it for a moment, and then it was gone. But there was no doubt about it. I had the pilot book and chart out from our last visit. I threw the helm over, skirted the reef and marked a course on the chart which would give us an extra wide berth. As luck would have it, dawn brought clearer visibility, favourable winds and we creamed into the harbour flying all the distress signals I could think of. We had a receiver but no transmitter on board. The Harbour Master was right there with his launch and had my wife in hospital in no time. Yes, it was appendicitis and as you can see, she made a full recovery.

'I invited the harbour master aboard that evening to share some of our Duty Free, as we had got to know him quite well two years ago. He complimented me on navigating into the harbour after a long voyage and arriving in such poor conditions. I told him how lucky it was that I saw the light in time, otherwise we would have piled up on the reef. Seeing the light at the last moment, I was able to take evasive action and showed him my chart with the course I had followed after seeing the light.

'The Harbour Master put down his Johnny Walker with a shaky hand and gave me a very strange look. Ladies and gentlemen, the Harbour Master took me out to the reef and this is a picture I took of the light the next day to show my wife in hospital.' He switched the slide projector back on and showed a rocky coastline, but with no light, just a pile of rubble.

'The Harbour Master explained that the light had been destroyed in a storm the previous winter. It had yet to be replaced. And yet the light I saw was exactly the signal that is marked in the pilot book which I recalled from our previous visit. It was the correct signal and it was in the right place. Here is the course I marked on the chart which brought us safely into harbour.' He held up a tattered chart for us all to see, and then shrugged his shoulders and smiled.

'If I had not seen whatever it was that I saw, we would have piled up on the reef. But I did see something that made me change course. Some may think of this as divine intervention. I can offer no logical explanation.' Neither could anybody else in that silent room.

Etiquette 2

Local loud mouth bothering you? Let Jack show you how this can be cured with just a slight dose of public ridicule

After the lecture broke up and tea and biscuits were served in ¼ inch thick cups, we all pressed around the heroic couple eager for further details of their fascinating cruising lifestyle. Unfortunately, a lofty fellow I knew slightly with a reedy voice and frame to match had taken it upon himself to protect the cruising couple from the rest of us. He knew that I and others crewed for Jack, who kept a motor cruiser on the Hamble. We had cruised the South Coast to Cornwall twice a year and had made several Channel crossings.

'These are stinkboat people. Stinkboats on rivers,' he warned, with a smile but not much humour. 'I don't know why they would come here anyway. They have no interest in feeling the tug of the tiller, the spray in their face. They could not tell you a jib from a jigger,' went on the Midland Masefield.

Jack turned to a member of the frustrated audience, 'Hornblower here, who is he and what sort of boat does he have? Got to be a square rigger to hear him. Where does he keep it?'

Somebody told him. Jack eased back into the melee. 'Hey Walter, when you are sailing full and by in a Force 5, thinking about pulling in a reef, with that tiller throbbing in your hand and feeling the spray in your face... On that Birmingham reservoir in that plastic dinghy of yours... I don't suppose you get out of sight of land often...?'

ETIQUETTE 3: THE FRENCH CONNECTION

One of your crew is threatened with extinction by a mountain of a drunken rugby player. What would Emily do? Jack did not have her book handy so had to think of something quick...

Nobody has ever replicated the English pub on foreign soil. I tried it myself in South America. We even had English beer flown in and served among a tasty collection of British Air Hosties. It was a financial success but it did not taste right. Maybe the beer was not warm enough or the chicken pies tasted of chicken. To get a real English pub flavour, you have to be in England and preferably somewhere in the West Country.

It was not the last night of one of our cruises, but it could have been, as we entered one of our favourite West Country harbourside hostelries and ordered refreshment for all hands. There was something different about the crowd tonight. A lot of big blokes in strange coloured jerseys. Some were talking funny. Apparently there was a major rugby tournament in the area. As this was billed as an 'International Event', and as Robert Morley lamented in *Those Magnificent Men*, it inevitably lead to an influx of foreigners. As well as totally foreign languages, like from the runners up at Trafalgar, there were snatches of English beginning with 'Christ, man...' and ending in 'eh?'... and guttural gibberish in between. Obviously, there were Seth Efricans among us.

I was feeling like most young blokes do in a pub after a few drinks, the funniest guy in the world, no pain and ten feet tall. Suddenly, there was an excruciating pain on the back of my left hand. Some blond haired refrigerator wearing a rugby shirt had stubbed his cigarette out on me. I was calm and reasonable and told the bastard he had done that on purpose and he had better apologise... or else.

He said, 'I apologise' in such a sneering manner and a *French accent*, I was horrified to see my right hand fling a full pint of best scrumpy into his face.

He was immediately surrounded by other refrigerators wearing rugby shirts demanding satisfaction in a strange language. I was wondering if duelling was still a legal pastime in France when he grabbed me and said, 'Outside!' There seemed little chance of talking my way out of this, what with the language barrier and all. Then I heard a voice which sounded like mine say, 'yep. Outside, let's go.'

I strode briskly into the outside air thinking that this hulk would cream me in one go and the pain would be limited until I woke up. The chill air and too much scrumpy brought further deliriums in a dose of Nationalistic fervour; I actually thought I could take on Monsieur Goliath and survive. I pranced around the car park, flinging Kung Fu gestures at the evening air, hoping to descrumpify my head. While I was doing some killer moves, a Renault started up behind me, belted out of the night, no lights, nearly took off my left leg and vanished. Where was my opponent? I wondered if I should go back in and remind this French giant he was supposed to come out and kill me when one of the crew appeared in the pub doorway, one hand beckoned me in, the other offered a fresh pint.

'Come on, Quirkie, you're getting behind.' As more glasses followed, and in the jovial company of good friends, the near death experience evaporated from memory.

Fast forward a quarter of a century, we were living in New York and a friend of ours was off to Europe on a sudden spur of the moment decision made after seeing the offer of a seriously discounted air fare. He did not know anyone there. Is there someone with whom we could put him in touch? Just so happened that one of the Old Crew had a sailing boat in the Med, would that do?

On his return, our very suntanned NY Mate regaled us with the best holiday, sorry, vacation, of his life. The OC member was about to embark on a three week cruise, would our NYM be interested in coming along?

One night in a French quayside bistro the OC asked NYM if Quirkie had ever told him about the French rugby player that was going to beat him to a pulp. Non? The OC related the story up until I confidently strode out of the pub to meet certain death.

'Then our skipper, Jack, went up to the French guy and politely asked him if he was a stranger here. He confirmed that he was, and Jack told him that often does that. That scraggy looking wimp with the glasses may look like a lean streak of wee and wind, but he is the Black Belt Champion of Wolverhampton. Last year he picked a fight in this very bar. They went outside and it was awful to watch. Not only did he put the poor rugby player in hospital and claim self defence, but his victim's knees were so damaged, the fellow missed playing for the *whole of the season*. At receiving such friendly advice from a considerate looking middle-aged gent, the Frog practiced the French Military's second favourite manoeuvre; The Retreat (the first being the surrender). He made a swift exit from a side door to his Renault.

My bold looking flight from the pub to meet my death and the phoney Kung Fu warm up exercise must have added to the illusion. I really cannot remember much of the latter part of that evening in the pub. Over-serving was a common problem in those places. They say that the one great thing in showbusiness is timing. But it's not often you wait twenty five years for a punchline.

Bodger's Bridal Blunder

John Quirk reflects on an eccentric, accident prone neighbour, an unusual boating incident and its aftermath...

Bodger was the only person I ever knew who was hit by a bridge. He was the consummate DIYer who spent a lifetime churning out Godawful hopeless projects and never learned anything from each ham-fisted failure. The large Bodger family lived in a vast unfinished ruin a couple of streets away. His cruel conversion of an innocent but slightly suspect ship's lifeboat brought ugliness to our waterways which was unmatched until the designers of the new superyachts cornered the market.

He was standing on the roofing-felt covered deck of his pride and joy, with a gaggle of family members presumably at the helm. He had his back to the scenery and did not see the stone arched bridge sneaking up on them. The fencing wire forestay snapped and the scaffold pole mast belted him over the back of the head and crushed him onto the wheelhouse. Bodger was saved by his own lousy workmanship when the whole structure collapsed onto his picnicking family in the cockpit. If Bodger was a little strange before this event, he certainly became more of a, let's say, 'character' afterwards.

Fast forward to the wedding of the first of Bodger's houseful of cello-shaped daughters. Bodger refused to outlay the cost of a hire car. With the prospect of a half dozen weddings in the offing, he had undertaken a full restoration of the family Austin to serve as the bridal car, and had invested in a gallon of a revolutionary quick drying black enamel and a new brush. Unfortunately, he ran out of time, again. And until he could remember where he had put all four mudguards, there was the niggling doubt about the car's legality on the road. Our neighbour Jack, with the neat Blackwater-built cruiser, gallantly offered to drive the bride and Bodger to the church in his Riley.

Bodger gave the rest of the bridal party a head start to get to the ceremony and looked about the junk-piled empty house. There was only Jack, the bride and Bodger in the place and it

would be empty for the next six hours. He felt he must take advantage of the situation. His eyes settled on the gallon tin of special quick drying paint in Wedding Car Black. He could not help himself. Bodger pried the lid off, and before he knew it he had painted the toilet seat a deep lustrous gloss.

All would have been well if the bride had not had a last minute attack of nerves. While Bodger was consoling a hysterical daughter, Jack ran up the stairs and handed a chain of petrol soaked rags from his fuel tank to the formally clad arm gesticulating from the modesty of the bathroom door. The bride used to choose her beauty products with great care as she had one of those 'delicate complexions'. Having half a gallon of Jet cut price petrol rubbed into her nether regions caused her to Vesuvius into fiery eruptions as far as the eye could see. Apart from that, she scrubbed up well, which is more than could be said for the wedding dress, now dalmationed with blotches of black paint.

Jack grabbed a pair of garden shears neatly filed on the hall table with a garden gnome and a WW2 stirrup pump. Most of the blackened bits of dress were deftly quarterised.

The bride and her proud father finally made their delayed trip down the aisle, reeking like an oil refinery. The bride appeared to walk a little stiffly and her complexion glowed like the back of a traffic jam. The bridal train resembled a diseased cockatoo, but for a quarter of a century none of the guests were aware of the drama that had unfolded.

'Doesn't she look lovely?' They all said.

Bodger had sworn Jack to an oath of secrecy. The story only came out when the bride was vigorously over served at her silver wedding anniversary, surrounded by surviving guests.

But this did clear up one odd memory of the wedding. Just before the last waltz, the MC announced an anonymous request for a little number that was dear to the hearts of the bride and her father.

'Take your partners for that popular dance of the Charleston era, ladies and gentlemen – the Black bottom!'

Lust at Low Ebb

What could be a more romantic setting for a tryst than the saloon of classic wooden boat, moored in the quiet seclusion of a Cornish cove? Quirkie recalls how true lust does not always run smoothly... A word to our younger readers, before all women came shrink wrapped in panty hose, they wore individual stockings. Yes, that's right. One on each leg

They lived maybe a mile apart but they might as well have been in different galaxies. She was a statuesque mini-skirted, garter-belted Avenger-booted vision of female delight that lived with

her parents and assorted broken-nosed rugby-playing brothers. It was said by some frightened off suitors that her ex-rugby-playing, ex-policeman father was reported to dust his only daughter down for fingerprints after returning from a late date.

He was a nervous inexperienced youth who lived a few streets away in that grimy Midland suburb, also with parents. During those swinging sixties, a few of his friends had escaped to live in cramped grease flavoured student digs, others solved the problem of romantic privacy by buying a Mini van (£360 for a brand new car!). Many a Mini rocked on its hydrolastic suspension in lovers' lanes, while our couple groped in the leaking claustro-phobic confines of the other passion of the lad's life – a smart, but aged open two-seater.

He could not imagine what attractions the stick insect 'Twiggy' models could hold when here was real curvaceous, value for money womanhood. She went in and out in all the right places. Particularly out.

It was with thoughts of those shapely stocking clad legs in mind that in the tiny back of his car, our dashing hero optimistically carried a corkscrew and a bottle of Blue Nun, wrapped up in an army surplus groundsheet. Sadly, throughout that cold soggy spring, all of the above remained unopened. Then oppor-tunity hammered on the door. He had enjoyed some coastal cruising on a neighbour's old sailing yacht. The boat was lying in Cornwall. Would some of last season's crew like to come down for a long weekend of refitting? Dormitory accommodation had been arranged which even met the approval of her Dad.

As the two seater leaked from every orifice, particularly from below, our hero spent the weekend before the Cornish expedition underWeeksealing the thing to death. After their first day working on the boat in glorious weather, the sun-seared crew retired to a jolly evening in the pub. Afterwards, our couple found themselves in the two seater, beneath a full moon, overlooking the cruiser in the seclusion of a cove of picture postcard beauty...

As they rowed out in the dinghy, the efflorescence of every oar stroke was a cascade of diamonds. They climbed aboard and found the batteries had been disconnected, the floor boards were up and the saloon bunks had been upended to make room for the sails, every bit of rope the ship possessed and about two dozen tins of paint. Nevertheless, in the darkness and jumble, things came together. Everybody seemed to know where to go and what to do.

It was several hours later that they found themselves dumped in a sudden heap on the cabin sole. The tide had gone out and the boat was on its ear at a 45 degree angle. (Romantic full moon = spring tides; highest high, lowest low.) They grabbed at their clothes and dressed by Braille. It was then that the heavens opened. This was not just Cornish rain, this would have set records in Cherrapunji. It sounded like a truck load of dried peas being dumped on the deck. There was no sign of the rain abating and dawn was starting to tint the Eastern sky. He steadied her into the flooded dinghy, she bailed while he rowed.

The weight of rainwater in the dinghy soon grounded it. Our hero leaped over the side, slipped and measured his length in the creek. He stumbled to his feet and began hauling his precious cargo ashore. He could not understand that despite the stinging cold of the rain, he felt strangely weak and light headed. The flooded dinghy and the curvaceous lust of his life would not move. It passed briefly through his mind that there may be advantages in these scraggy lightweight 'Twiggy' types after all. Eventually he suggested that instead of sitting there complaining that her feet were wet, she might as well give him a hand in dragging this damned boat. He tried to steady her as she got out but in that treacherous shell studded mud, they both wound up sprawling in the ooze. She stormed off, well, squelched off towards the two seater. In their ardent haste, it had been left open. The new underseal had done a grand job, she opened the door and water and the seat cushions poured over her feet... The dorm was less than half a mile away.

The next day, as the brilliant afternoon drew to a close and the crew were contemplating the five hour drive back, one of his friends noted that the love of his life seemed to have left early. Didn't he see her leaving with that mate of theirs? The one with Mini van?

Our hero explained that his car was caught with its roof down and the seats were sodden, and she had to leave early anyway...

The friend deduced the bleeding obvious, that the flames of passion had been well and truly extinguished and asked, 'So how long did it last between you and miss... long legs?'

'I can tell you exactly,' he replied, eyeing the distance between the yacht and the quay.
'About 75 feet.'

HYPOTHETICAL 1

Quirkie faces a bit of a situation when a salvage operation goes slightly wrong

Do you remember those Hypotheticals that Des Sleightholme used to run in *Yachting Monthly*? You know, the ordinary little everyday seamanship problems that would crop up in everybody's cruising career... 'It's midnight and raining like hell, you are dragging anchor on a lee shore in a rising gale, with a dead engine and flat batteries. The rats have eaten your halyards, the chain is kinked in the hawse and you can't get at it because your mother in law is jammed in the heads with dysentery...'

Well, try this... You are 6 miles off the coast of an island in the Seychelles in an ageing 11 foot inflatable. You have been diving on a wreck, liberating port holes and other yellow metal which you are taking back to a Chinese trader's workshop, and whittling them into rudder fittings for a yacht your mate is building. (And you still think I make this stuff up?) Your mate hauls up half a sabre-toothed porthole and flings it into the inflatable. There is nothing to wrap it in and you suggest that it might be better to tow the thing on a line at a safe distance. Your wimpy idea is vetoed and you watch it roll around with the horror of seeing a hedgehog running amok in a condom factory. It touches the side. There's a bit of a hiss. He starts the outboard, tells you to cast off from the buoyed line secured to the wreck. You do, and he clunks into gear. Nothing happens. The shear pin has sheared. He hands you the pump which is a macramé of perished bicycle puncture patches.

'Just keep pumping,' he grins, pointing to the Island. 'We should blow ashore soon.'

Conversationally, you enquire how far we are from the coast of Africa. 'Bits of it are only a thousand miles away. Why?' You point out the wind direction. The South East Trades are blowing you there. Away from the island, towards Africa. His smile slides overboard.

The first jolt of sheer terror nearly filled my wet suit. We realised we had to get some form of shear pin to function. There were no signs of any tools on board, of course, and nothing that looked like a shear pin. The spare ones I had brought over were safely ashore in the skipper's Mini Moke. Then something happened which I am told occurs frequently to other people's brains but rarely to mine – an idea happened.

We stopped the engine and I went over the side with a diving knife and worried the cotter pin out of the spinner. It was corroded to fuse wire thickness, no shear pin potential there. A plastic bucket was held as a Long Stop, under a cupped hand to catch the bits of broken pin, the freely spinning prop was eased off the shaft. No microsurgery was ever performed with the breath holding precision of our shearpinectomy. Three shining pieces, each more valuable to us than the Kohinoor diamond, plopped into a grateful palm. The middle piece was longer than the two outer ones. We reassembled them in a revised order so that the breaks were in a different position.

Very, very gently, the skipper started the engine and we held our breath as we crept back to the island with me working the disintegrating pump while our once proudly firm inflatable wilted like... well, gentle reader, you can supply your own simile here...

Quite frequently in my boating career I seem to be leaping into the shallows, hugging the beach and promising never ever to go out on that wet stuff again. Well, not until the next time. The amazing thing was that after this display of foresight and seamanship, our skipper made a very sound job of completing his yacht, took his family on an extended and successful Indian Ocean cruise, moved to Australia and eventually sold the boat at a profit.

Sometimes life just isn't fair, is it?

So, for the last few decades, while the eternal optimist in some folk has caused them to carry certain items in the deep recesses of their wallets in case of, er, unexpected events, the pessimist in me carries shear pins and snippets of wire coat hangers for the same reason.

Besides this dose of paranoia, I have another souvenir of the Seychelles, a bank note of the period. The designer was supposed to have featured all the attractions the Islands had to offer, you can see the sailing schooners and rocky scenery, but do those palms behind the Queen's head really spell out what I think they do?

Hypothetical 2

The Quirkie craft's maiden voyage is on a quiet shallow lake. What could go wrong?

OK, let's suppose that you and your housemate have each built a 16 foot plywood Sunfish on your kitchen table in the old East African farmhouse in which you are living. You take the first boat for a test run with the mate, who is a structural engineer and finished his first.

You decide to test it on one of the Lakes in the Great Rift Valley, throw it on the roof of the faithful old Peugeot wagon and off you go. It floats! Wow, great. Now let's rig the lateen sail on those aluminium irrigation pipe spars. The engineer does not trust the drawings, which showed an unstayed mast. He has added chainplates and neat twists of fencing wire to the masthead. No turnbuckles. With the help of a paddle, you catch the gentle breeze, which wafts you out to the middle of the lake. Then it plays with you, like a cat does with a captured mouse. Calm then squall, then calm, all come off the sun heated hills. Then wallop, *that* was a squall! It all happens in a millisecond.

The boom belts across at teeth height, the BSc gets knocked over one side, you fall backwards over the other. The Sunfish is lying on its ear and while you are trying to think where you went wrong, the hollow spars fill with water, the BSc grabs the upended side... and the boat turns upside down. You swim over and reach for the dagger board to lever the boat upright but it sinks down into the trunk. You try to pull it up, but for some reason, it will not move. You can tell now by the feel of the upturned hull that the mast is drilling for oil in the muddy lake bed, about eight feet down.

'Don't worry,' grins the BSc, 'we must be drifting ashore, that rock is getting closer.' And so it is. There appears to be a low slab just above the surface you had not noticed before and it is definitely getting closer. But if the mast is nailed to the bottom, we are obviously not moving, so why is this rock coming nearer? Perhaps because this rock is not a rock. This rock is a hippo. Most people think of a hippo as a large amiable waterlogged pig, but not quite. Your average porker does not have teeth like this. And they have a set of jaw muscles to match. I once saw the result of a territorial scrap between a rhino and a hippo. It was a draw. But the fatally gored hippo did a neat job of biting through the rhino's neck. Those teeth, in a ton or two of wet pork, were now approaching us.

Send your answer to getting out of this Hypothetical Mess to *Practical Boat Owner* and see if you can win a set of plastic fenders. Also, I would be interested to know what the correct procedure is.

We were sitting on the upturned bottom eyeing Hippo rock when we realised there was a further problem. The BSc had made a few modifications to the Sunfish design, which included cockpit storage lockers for essential equipment. You could now get four longneck 26 oz Pilsner bottles in each side. But these lockers were not watertight. Nor were the 'watertight' bulkheads along the hull. As the boat filled, the only buoyancy would be the flotation of the plywood itself. I thought I should mention this.

'Good Heavens!' exclaimed the BSc. 'That means that we will be taking on 16 x 2 x 0.5 x 62.427 pounds of water,' doing the rough mental arithmetic in his head for the volume of the hull and the cubic feet of water it could hold.

'That's roughly 998.832 pounds. We will never lift that.' It was time to lose the mast. We reached over and began to fumble with the fencing wire shrouds. Our hands had wrinkled as if we had been too long in the bath, but in sheer desperation, we ignored the shredding flesh and eventually had the wire detached from the hull.

OK, let's get the mast out of the hull, turn it over and we can get back onto the boat the right way and try to bale it. No pole dancers have ever done such a strenuous routine as we did to grab the mast with both hands while under the Sunfish and to shoulder the waterlogged hull upward. I think it was a combination of driving the mast deeper as well as lifting, that meant we were able to get the hull free from the mast.

We managed to get the dagger board down and used it to lever the boat the right way up. It floated with the deck level with the water. Alas, a bailer had not been considered essential equipment along with the beer. But even these mad dog Englishmen did not go out in the noon day sun without hats. These were used to bale the cockpit and the constant trickles that oozed in there from the rest of the hull. Fortunately, our porcine companion was keeping his distance, two little islands of eyes held us under observation. But we were a mile or so from the shallow reedy shore, we could not extricate the mast from the mud, and the sails and spars were all attached to this. Also, so were we. The mainsheet stopper knot was not the sailor's figure of eight, but a Gordian jumble which was now waterlogged and unravelable. A knife had also not been considered essential equipment either. How are we going to get out of this?

Well, as you will have guessed, it's quite obvious really. We were rescued by the Russian Navy. A distant hum and a dark blue hull were approaching. This was our good mate Laurie Balabanoff in *Bluebell*. Laurie's family had not been invited to join in the 1917 Russian Revolution and left for East Africa. I had helped him fit out a 20 foot moulded timber hull, in which he was out every weekend maintaining his position as the champion fisherman on the Lake. Laurie had seen our predicament and at his arrival, the waterlogged rock seemed to subside.

From the safety and stability of *Bluebell*, we soon had the mast, sails and spars aboard, the Sunfish in tow and were heading back to shore.

A couple of Commandments to learn from all this: apart from possibly taking an elephant gun with you while sailing in such conditions, always carry a bailer *attached* to the boat and don't leave home without your sailor's knife.

My Sunfish was completed shortly after this event, with no mods to the standard design. It was taken to the coast for the launch and it was dark by the time we were rigged and in the water. I was impatient to go for a test sail within the lagoon and pushed off the beach. The Trade wind was a warm caress and filled the sail so it billowed into a rigid arc of perfection. The Sunfish ploughed a hissing furrow through the sea. Everything seems faster at night,

particularly at sea... And then we were flying. The spray was warm and thick with salt which crusted on my skin. It added to the exhilaration of that magic ride. This was the same wind that had blown seamen over the centuries to discover the whole of the world. I wanted to hug this moment to me and never let it go. It was a magic experience that has stayed with me over the years.

So when we experience a few upsets; sinkings, fouled anchors, groundings, getting lost, little stuff like that, it is memories like these that keep us going. We know that they are still out there, ready for us to enjoy.

Out of Africa 1

Leaving what the old explorers referred to as the Dark Continent? Can't take your money with you? Quirkie inspects some floating assets

Living in immediate post-Colonial Africa was like being in a first class cabin in the *Titanic*. So far, so good. But you knew you had to get into a lifeboat some time and it was best to do this at a time of your choosing rather than wait for that midnight (or more usually 4am) knock on the cabin door.

The problem was, if you had been remitting the small amount allowed for savings out of the country there was no way – no *legal* way – you could take any more with you. However, a number of the departing expatriate escaper's club had built boats using their local funds and went on extended cruises from which they never returned. (See also 'Hypothetical 1'). They often had names blatantly suggesting their purpose, such as *Escaper* or *Kwa Heri* (Goodbye). There were a few under construction in secluded locations, which I checked out with their owner or builders.

The butt jointed rubbing strake and wavey waterline were a giveaway . . .

The first was a plywood effort based on a Maurice Griffiths design which was approaching completion outside the owner's rented house. On approach, you could see the builder was no threat to Camper & Nicholsons. The butt jointed rubbing strake and wavy waterline were a giveaway, as was the allotment shed colour scheme. The owner had practiced taking sights with his plastic sextant with the navigating officers on the bridge of a ship coming out from UK, and was supremely confident about the voyage.

'Of course, these Griffiths designs are alright for the East Coast, but for an ocean going vessel, I had to make a lot of modifications.' (This guy is telling MG how to design a boat?) 'First of all, you need more headroom. I raised the cabin roof. Bit more beam too. Not enough room for me, my wife, the baby and the ayah...'

'So you will be taking a baby and a nursemaid with you?'

'Of course. My wife can't do it all and you don't think I am going to be looking after the baby, do you? I will be skipper.'

When asked if he used local craftsmen to help him with the construction, he loftily claimed it was all his own work and would not let any of the locals near the thing.

Once he had shown me such nautical details as the space he had contrived for the washing machine, I looked around. It was, without doubt, the worst amateur effort I had ever seen. Instead of bolting the chain plates through the hull and reinforcing pads to spread the load, he had fixed them to the hull with brass screws. He had aimed them at the edge of a plywood bulkhead. And missed. Where the screws projected into the cabin, what looked like a badly made hornets' nest was in fact where he had liberally gobbed over the screw ends with plastic wood. I made a gentle retreat, without touching the structure of the boat, fearful of a collapse. I heard later that he had launched the thing in the Indian Ocean and made it to the next port down the coast. Here it was hoisted aboard a ship as deck cargo for the remainder of the voyage to the UK. I hope he reached there by Bonfire Night as that was surely all it could be used for.

The second vessel was built by a departing civil servant who had bought the plans of a Dutch-designed 40 foot steel yacht, and taught himself welding. He had also done an immense amount of research on anti-corrosion treatments, which resulted in a competent construction of this strange angular craft that only a Dutchman could love. When I saw it, it had already begun to rust and the intensely researched paint job had turned some very peculiar colours. Although he had followed the original hull design, he too had made modifications below. The

saloon contained a large gas water heater over berths that were towering above the cabin sole. He lifted the port side berth top to reveal a full sized bath.

'My wife would not come with me unless she could have her daily bath,' he announced while opening the starboard berth to reveal a welded-in water tank. There was no point in explaining to him that a bath requires 20 gallons of water, which weighs 200 pounds and that he had all his water on one side of the hull so he would need to compensate for the reduced weight as the water was consumed.

I later saw this vessel after he had launched it at the coast. It was rusted from stem to stern and had blended nicely with its jungle environment.

Do not get the impression that the whole of East Africa was inhabited by selected white idiots who could not make a living in their homeland... But it had its share.

Harry, another fellow I met, had for years planned a sailing retirement aboard his own boat. He had extensive experience sailing the last of the old British trading ketches and a vast collection of books and models of commercial sailing craft from all over the world. He had actually gone to Tahiti and been shown over William Albert Robinson's wonderful *Varua* by the owner. This was the rig for Harry. He wanted a brigantine with staysails between the masts and decided to build one about 55 feet long in ferro-cement. I helped him loft a hull design he had in stock, and soon this massive structure grew beneath the tin roof shade structure. Harry had been shot down in Hurricanes three times before his 21st birthday. The last time, the glycol engine coolant burned his face. When he was in shorts on the building site, you could see where all the skin grafts had been taken from to patch up his face. Unfortunately, Harry suffered a series of strokes, which left him very frustrated at not being able to communicate. Sadly, the last one was fatal.

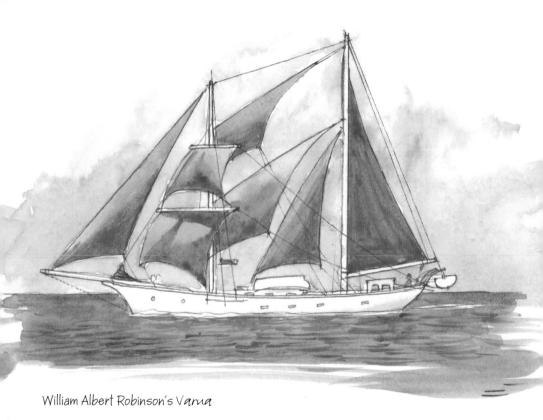

William Albert Robinson's *Varua*

The fourth boat was built by a character that embodied everything you ever imagined a between the Wars colonial adventurer could be. MacDonald left Scotland in 1918 for East Africa where he became a gold miner, coffee and tea planter. He farmed in Kenya's Happy Valley during the days of 'White mischief', when the national sport was wife swapping. During the War, he designed and built a floating crane for the Admiralty that could hoist the heaviest guns out of navy ships. This involved first building his own dry dock on the beach and the

'... and she had a pair like this...'
Mac discusses exhaust manifolds . . .

total project was achieved with native labour who Mac trained on the job. I am sure he had been a lead player in the Happy Valley First XI. When I met him, he had recently remarried and had promised his German born bride a cruise of the Mediterranean and the European waterways. They were both pushing 70 but Mac had the craggy good looks of an agricultural Louis Mountbatten, a regal mane of grey hair, dark eyebrows and twinkling, roving eyes in Paul Newman blue. He was still serious competition. You did not leave your girlfriend unattended with Mac around.

He had seen an article about a McBride designed 35 foot motor sailer that had won a competition for being an ideal boat in which to undertake a cruise around the British Isles. He had an engineering workshop and a Kuke labour force that he had trained over many years to his own high standards of skills. They were more at home building in steel rather than timber so he compromised and used composite construction. 'Good enough for the *Cutty Sark*,' he noted. She had galvanised steel angle frames to which the carvel planking was hook bolted. He had followed the design perfectly and the result was a very professional rugged motor sailer. He had marinised a Rootes three cylinder turbocharged diesel. It had three cylinders but was 'flat' design with six pistons (!) and it fitted snugly beneath the wheel house floor.

The boat would be ideal for the temperate climate of Europe. Perhaps a little light on sitting out space, but I am sure Mac would have turned part of the aft deck into a cockpit accessible from the aft galley if this were required. After I left the country, the boat was trucked to the coast in preparation for Mac and crew to deliver her up the Med, via the Red Sea and Suez, where his wife would join him. Then his stepson asked if he could borrow the boat for a few days before they went.

Another Nautical Commandment is 'Thou shalt not use sisal rope for anchoring where there is coral about'. You can guess what happened. She drifted ashore and although she survived, the replacement of a whole side of her bent ribs was a major job. Mac had sold his workshop and no longer had the facilities, nor I suspect, the enthusiasm for the task.

I was working down on the idyllic island of Lamu off the Kenya coast before electricity and tourists got to the place. It was straight out of *Arabian Nights* at the time. Who would have thought that I would later have sons and the place would become trendy enough for one of them to spend his honeymoon there? A friend of mine (Rob Wiseman, where are you?) brought electric power to the place by installing a couple of generators. He soon found that power demand was miniscule and brief with a massive surge at dusk for maybe two minutes; just long enough for the locals to turn on the lights, find the matches and light the oil lamps.

One afternoon, into the channel sailed a vision of delight that stood my corpsuckles on edge. She looked like a Bristol Channel Pilot Cutter whose mother had mated with a dhow. Her blue sails blended with the impossibly deep blue of the sky. A couple of British architects based in Uganda had commissioned a local dhow builder to build them a forty something foot vessel based on pilot boat lines. The keel and ballast were ironwood, her topsides were a local hardwood and were oiled, which brought out the rich mahogany colour. There was no engine; she was cutter rigged with three headsails. The main was huge, rigged bawley-style and brailled

to the mast. The swinging mainsheet block was the size of, and as lethal as, a cannon ball. Including the suit of blue imported sails, she had cost them £2,800. This was like stepping into the nineteenth century, being able to order your own affordable pilot cutter.

She was built by eye, argument and stick marks in the sand. The workmanship was a little agricultural with all grown frames, but that price does not get you much fine finishing beyond the adze stage. But she was solid, had a barrel of room below and felt like a real ship.

The owners departed for a thousand mile shakedown cruise to the Seychelles, then on to UK via Brazil where they attempted to start a boat yard building hulls in ferro-cement. I read about this later in a women's magazine. I also saw the vessel advertised for sale in UK at over three times the building cost. Hmm. So it *can* be done...

Out of Africa 2

Quirkie plots the Great Escape

Further research into home-made boats leaving Africa revealed a family who built a 40 foot plywood Piver trimaran (remember them?) and sailed against the Trades to New Zealand. The remarkable thing about this was they took their infirm 90-year-old granny along for the ride. She reportedly enjoyed the whole trip and knitted her way across the Indian Ocean.

But this ferro-cement stuff intrigued me. It was being pushed along by *Yachting Monthly* at the time as the future of DIY boatbuilding. As an architect, I understood about thin ferro structures and recall Luigi Nervi's demonstration yacht. This construction suited my particular circumstances.

I was completing a game viewing lodge on 25,000 acres which had failed as a goat farm. The overseas development company owed me money that I was unlikely to see. This meant I could not roll up to 'Dhows R Us' and say 'same again'. I kept on with the lodge project because it was going to be managed by an international hotel group and I wanted to do a good job for them. My building team were a few Asian 'mistris', or foremen, and a horde of barefoot African tribesmen. The amount owed to me easily covered the cost of materials and labour for a 40 foot ferro-hull and a modest fit-out. But if I built one, how would I get it to the sea? There were only game trails linking this site to the outside world. The trick with game lodges is to build them from materials from the site itself as other deliveries could only be trucked in during the dry season.

While surveying part of the site for an airstrip, one of the team tripped over a piece of old iron in the long grass. It was a railway line. Not just a piece of line but a whole railway track. It had been built to supply General Smut's army in WW1 when the Allies and the Germans successfully avoided each other for years, and it had remained largely unused since. It was still connected to the main coast line, and yes, I could get a train to the site! It seemed like a sign from above. I measured a railway low loader wagon. Thirty nine feet was the maximum length, but if the overhangs were above the adjacent wagons, this length could be exceeded to 45 or 46 feet. There were no serious width or height restrictions; it was a single track with no bridges over it. Now what was the best hull to suit these criteria?

With this delicious thought buzzing in my head, I found myself on one of the first flights to the Seychelles to look at a cliff top site for a resort. There are 92 islands in the chain, not all are uninhabited, but those that are, are supplied by a fleet of wooden sailing schooners. These are about 45 to 50 feet long and they take paying passengers on their annual schooner races. Walking around those steady wide decks, snug behind knee high bulwarks while receiving the gentle blast of a Force 5 Trade wind, blew any thoughts of a more 'yachty' design out of the contest. I wanted a ship. And they also used home-made fittings that we could fabricate at Mac's workshop. The mast and spars were fresh out of the ground trees and the largest sail was around 400 square feet, reckoned to be the largest area one bloke could handle without hurting himself.

In my collection of 'boaty' designs, Harry had given me the lines of a typical New England schooner hull, a chunky full bodied design that could stand the heavy displacement of a cement hull and deck. There is lots of room on board, you may as well make yourself comfortable, you are not going anywhere in a hurry in a boat like this. If I could get my double elephant (40 x 26 inch) drawing board in, then I could earn a living wherever I was.

I lofted the hull at 39 feet on the keel on reclaimed plywood shutter boards. I found ways to get ferro-cement details and supplies into finishing the lodges to determine the skill of my barefoot artisans. I also made test panels to establish the strength of various mixes and water contents. The barefoot brigade soon learned the gentle art of pipe bending and we had a set of frames, tack welded with zig-zag reinforcing steel.

The 'Barefoot Boatyard' was discreetly set up with frames erected the right way up alongside the railway line at a height to suit heaving onto a low loader. The frames were soon wired

I did not want a yacht – I wanted a ship . . .

together with steel rods at three inch centres. Instead of using the usual eight layers of chicken wire for reinforcement, I ordered a truckload of coffee tray wire. This is a fine galvanised welded mesh made for drying coffee beans. It is superior to the other stuff and you need fewer layers. Interestingly, not only had my Barefoot Boatbuilders never seen the sea, a few even doubted its existence. They thought this was another one of those fanciful white men's tales they had heard, such as there are parts of the world where Europeans do the washing up and mow their own lawns... And Governments pay you for not working... Who could believe such nonsense?

Meanwhile, back at the lodge site, we were about to do the final fit-out when it was discovered that a major chunk of the club funds had gone missing. My completion budget was slashed to a fraction of what was needed. How do I get out of this one?

Then I heard of two German art teachers who had been driving through Africa. They noticed that many of the traditional African arts and craft skills were being lost. They set up a small craft school and out of their own pocket, gave free meals to their students. This attracted a crowd of street orphans who were soon turning out beautiful sculptures, carvings, metalwork, woodwork, fabrics, enamel and fine paintings. The sale of these funded the building of a workshop and paid the kids a pocket money wage. I reviewed the lodge requirements with the Germans and told them the reduced budget. They thought it was a fortune. We reworked the fit-out to suit the craft school skills and off we went. I redesigned much of the fit-out and furniture to use sisal poles. These had never been used before and had been burned as waste. We acquired an entire field full for 50p.

We had 400 street kids learning traditional skills and they produced magnificent work, which enabled us to open the lodge on time and on budget. Things would now be looking good for the fit-out of the ferro-hull. We had built dormitories for the students and they opened a shop selling the best artwork and souvenirs in town. They were taught not only craft skills but how to run a business, keep records etc. The art teachers who had created the whole enterprise received the traditional reward of a grateful government. The pre-dawn knock on the door, and deportation for corrupting the minds of their youths with thoughts of 'Colonialism and Imperialism'. But these were Germans; they had not had a colony since 1917! Soon the bush telegraph word was out that for my association in this project, I could be next. The shop and workshop were closed down and 400 kids went back on the street. This was unusual. This was ideology gone mad. Normally, some government official or a relative would plunder it, not pay the staff and run it into the ground. As long as the African continent is run by stupid, greedy, narrow minded crooks like this, it will remain a basket case demanding to be supported by the rest of us.

I rushed back to the lodge for the official opening. The hull was almost ready for plastering but there was still a huge amount of work to do. How long had I got to finish it before the possible knock on the door? The president of the hotel management company had arrived for the opening and looked around at the magnificent fit-out which had been created by the now defunct craft school and its off the street artisans.

'You like working in jungles, don't you?' Yep, that's me.

'Got another jungle for you if you are interested.'

'Yes please. Where?'

'New York City. Come and be our architect. When can you leave? I will send you a plane ticket.'

I farewelled my bare foot friends and told them I was leaving but would be going in an 'ndegi ya chuma' (metal bird) and would not need the boat. They were welcome to all the materials from the hull and could use them for chicken houses. One of the lads who spoke excellent English got a job in the Lodge, taught himself German and the last I heard was the resident manager of the largest hotel on the coast. Not often you get good news stories out of Africa.

I also found that a local 'Mr Chips', a maths master of a prestigious boy's school, could do a great conjuring trick. He could make a briefcase of local money disappear, and reappear overnight in a European bank account in any currency. Mine woke up in Spain as British Quids.

I never returned to this part of Africa. However, in letters from Mac, he told stories of a strange structure not far from the lodges which will surely baffle future explorers. It appears my barefoot boatbuilder mates took the offer to use the hull materials for chook pens, but they did not pull it apart. Somewhere in the African bush, he said, there is a tribe that keeps its chickens in what looks like an inverted schooner hull. And the bottom is thatched.

Not sure about this. Particularly when his directions to get there say, 'Turn left at the elephant's graveyard'...

Do you think this is another of his traveller's tales?

BRIEF ENCOUNTER

How many NY shrinks does it take to save a runaway dinghy? Alright, why wouldn't any of them help Tom and Quirkie when their only link with the shore headed out to sea? The answer may surprise you...

'Here,' said cockney Tom in my ear in a stage whisper that was heard from stem to glistening stern of fifty something foot of *Chris Craft*. 'You realise that not only are we the only limeys on board, except for the skipper and his wife, but we are the only ones that aren't bleeding shrinks?'

He was dead right. The owner/skipper's wife was a psychiatrist in NYC and she had invited a dozen or so of her workmates and other halves to see the Cavalcade of Sail on Long Island Sound, celebrating America's bicentenary in 1976. (Why do so many shrinks marry shrinks? Is it because nobody else will have them?)

Tom and I had been signed on at the last minute by the skipper as deckhands and general help. To get the *Chris Craft* at a good location in the Sound, all guests had to be ferried out to the boat by dinghy from a jetty on the Westchester shore where no berthing was allowed. This had taken more effort and self control than getting the troops onto Omaha Beach.

How Tom had graduated from selling lamps from a barrow in London's East End to becoming the Darling of Lighting for Broadway Theatres has never been fully explained, but the journey was strewn with memorable anecdotes. He took a break from one of these, and dribbled off into speechless admiration of the sheer beauty of the soft summer evening, watching the unique splendour of the World's Finest Tall ships slicing glittering wakes through a blazing sunset. He even put down his can of ale and surveyed the scene with a professional eye.

'Nice drop of lighting. Innit?'

The guests were not distracted by such trivialities. They swapped case histories, drink in one hand, cigarette in the other, and shouted Martini-flavoured opinions into each others' faces.

'You call that a phobia? That's not a phobia. Lemme tell you 'bout a phobia.' They proceeded to out-phobia each other as this magnificent procession glided past, no doubt filled with crews who were brimming with phobias from top to toe. If only they knew, help was half a cable away.

Tom and I probably stood out in jeans and T-shirts; the male guests all wore a relaxed nautical uniform of striped, washable, ice-cream vendor-style suits, wide ties under buttoned down collars and polished black brogues with soles as thick as divers' boots.

The ladies wore the polyester plumage of tropical birds. The largest one of the species swooped on Tom. She inhabited a stretch kaftan with a technicolour rainforest theme. She looked like Maui.

'Oi just LURVE the worrah, don't you?' gushed this modest lady. 'When Oi was a girl you couldn't keep me outta the worrah. Swim? Tell me abourrit. I won every life saving medal that was ever minted.'

The warm night closed in and it was dark when we dropped anchor. There was not a breath of wind, the *Chris Craft* was as steady as a car park and the sea was black glass. Maui laid down maybe her tenth lipstick encrusted glass and declared that the motion was getting to her.

'Can't understand it. Oi was always such a good sailor. I mean, like really, really good.' This was a signal to begin the task of decanting the guests. Fortunately, the *Chris Craft* was equipped

with a proper set of companion steps with a small grating at the base. Mr and Mrs Maui were first. It took three of us to gently steady her swaying bulk into the dinghy and stow her on the centre seat. Her husband, who appeared to have been made on a scale ¾ to that of his wife, was forward, and our skipper climbed in aft and cranked the Seagull. They rattled shorewards beneath a night sky that was studded with stars and the moon lay on the mirror of the water like a silver tray. Mrs Maui appeared to notice the surroundings for the first time.

'This is so bootiful! Look at the moon. I wanna take it home with me.'

She pushed her scale model husband aside and leaned over the bow to scoop up the moon's reflection from the surface of the sea. This sudden shift in ballast caused the dink's bow to dive underwater and inhale a hullfull of Long Island Sound. It went under in seconds.

It appeared that our lifesaving heroine had forgotten how to swim. With a scream not heard since the last Tarzan film, she thrashed the water like an early hovercraft. Her husband and the skipper tried to approach her while keeping clear of those flailing arms and grabbed a few yards of floating kaftan which was spreading like a psychedelic oil slick. Then an amazing discovery was made; the water was about four feet deep. As the two of the dinghy crew struggled to beach Maui in the shallows, Tom grabbed my drinking arm.

'Ere, the bleeding dinghy's getting away, innit?'

Ballasted by the drowned outboard, the dink was now vertical in the water, with just the tip of the forward buoyancy chamber showing. It presented the maximum area to the strengthening ebb. It was rapidly making its escape between lines of moored boats to the open sea.

'If we don't save that bloody boat, we will be stuck on this ship of fools for the rest of our naturals.' He pulled off his T-shirt and called to the male guests. 'Oi, we need a bit of help here, we got to get this dink back.' They burst into action. One loosened his tie, another looked for a place to park his Martini. The dink was now making alarming progress and would soon be out of sight in the darkness. Tom and I shucked shirts and jeans and were down to our M&S briefs. I remember a flash of Tom's electric blue and I was in my canary yellow period. Our volunteers froze into immobility. Then we were over the side and chasing our salvation. We were exhausted when we laid hands on the fibreglass and it just carried us with it. We tried grabbing at fenders as we passed the procession of moored boats but they were too thick and shiny to hold on to. Tom began knocking on the passing hulls asking if anyone was home. Finally, a sleep befuddled mess of white hair peered over a gunwale and asked if we were alright.

'Oright? 'Course we're orright,' said Tom calmly. 'We always take the dinghy for a swim this time of night don't we?... No we're NOT alright! Bloody drownin' we are. Give us a rope!'

A bundle of heavy anchor warp crashed over Tom's head, its coils embraced him like a killer octopus in one of those old RKO Radio films. We secured the runaway dink and the elderly gent, stopping only to wrap his deck chair striped pyjamas in a woolly dressing gown, stepped over the opposite of his boat into an outboard runabout. He began towing the dinghy by the bow eye with us clinging to the side. He called out 'Hang on!' and suddenly opened the throttle. The runabout heaved itself onto the plane, and the dink – with us hanging on – followed with the water in the dink surging over the transom. We were bailed in an instant. Mind you, the ensuing tsunami caused a few wide awake comments from inside the hulls that had made no reply to our earlier tapping. Serves them right.

We arrived back in time to help quell the mutiny. The skipper was back aboard facing the sort of crowd scene you usually see outside US Embassies around the world. ('Death to America … and by the way, can I get a visa?')

The guests were panicking to get ashore. The dinghy had already sunk once, so presumably this was a character flaw and it could do it again. Any traditions of ladies having priority in lifeboats from *Titanic* days were sadly overlooked.

Order was finally established, the last Martini-filled ice cream suit and polyester plumage were rowed ashore and we returned the *Chris Craft* to its distant mooring.

Tom called me the next day.

'Here, I've just had a call from the skipper's wife thanking us for last night. I told her what I thought of her shrinky mates not helpin' us to save the dink. She told us why they wouldn't. You will never guess why… It was our knickers! She said it was when we were down to our Marks and Sparks briefs that they all bleeding froze. She said she could see what was happening. All the blokes were wearing those flappy 'Fruit Of The Loom' shorts that come halfway down your calf. And of course they all have undershirts and suspenders to hold their socks up. This crowd had been lecturing the world on phobias and here they were, scared shirtless at being seen shirtless and in their unmentionables.

Who has the underwear phobia?

'Here, you should write this up sometime. And I got a title for you. Remember that old black and white Noël Coward film where Trevor Howard and Celia Johnson meet at the railway station…?'

BOATING: WEST AFRICAN STYLE

Ever feel official rules and regulations are interfering with your boating and personal freedom? Pollies out of touch? Getting grief from the Greenies? Can't even throw your tea leaves overboard? Thinking of giving it all up and sailing away to some tropical paradise? It could be worse... Quirkie recalls an alternative. It may seem slightly amusing from your armchair, but all this really happened...

In the 1900s the average life expectancy of a male living in the US was 41 years. It is always distressing to hear that today there are some countries where the male life span is the same. It is particularly distressing to read this as you arrive in one of them on your 41st birthday.

My company had been approached and asked to find a site and design and operate an international standard hotel in this West African country. This week's dictator felt that once they had a five star hotel, they could automatically host a future OAU Meeting (Organisation of African Unity – it no longer exists.)

Not only did I arrive on my birthday, it was also Independence Day and the country was celebrating 23 years since the end of Colonial Rule. The story was that the new African President told the departing European Nation that he wanted his country back to the state it was before the white man arrived. Apparently he got his wish; not a telephone nor light bulb was left intact...

As a Guest of the Government, I was greeted at the airport with traditional hospitality. This means being jabbed in the ribs by rifles of sullen, threatening troops with demands for money.

The ends of the barrels were the only clean part of these greasy weapons, worn bright by regular polishing against arrivals to the country.

I was then rescued by a Government minder, bundled into a 23-year-old Peugeot and given a grand tour of the Capital. Only two buildings had been (almost) completed in those 23 years. First was a bolt together imported 'hotel' where I paid one of the staff twice the daily wage ($1) to stand guard on the working air conditioning unit to my room and make sure it was not swapped for a dud. Nobody worked on Independence Day so it was the following morning we left the Meccano Motel and dodged the potholes to meet Government Officials. This bone shaking ride took us past the other almost complete building, The People's Palace, a gift from those generous folks in North Korea, eager to share their wealth. It was completely ringed by armed troops.

'What are all those armed guards outside for?' I asked.

'To keep the people out.'

The Government offices looked like one of those war zones you see in newsreels. But this place was not at war. For the last 23 years, there had been nobody there to instruct that maintenance needs to be done. The lifts died a generation ago and the concrete stairs had been somehow destroyed so that only the steel angle nosings were left above a pulverised concrete ramp. It resembled the scree around Kilimanjaro. You climbed up using the handrail like a ski lift. I was led along a debris strewn corridor to a stifling shabby conference room and introduced to a dozen or so bored looking officials, none of whom would have seen a 41st birthday.

MINISTRY OF WORKS

Four of them at the end of the table barely looked up from a dog-eared collection of ragged papers they were studying. It was Mercedes Benz brochure, so battered a bag lady would have ignored it.

I asked them why they wanted to host an OAU meeting.

'When we hold one here, we all get a Mercedes.'

'?'

'That is what happens. Hotels get built. We want a conference centre. And we each get a Mercedes.'

'Who builds them? Who pays for the cars?'

Lots of nasal exploration, slow shrugging and wiping faces with palms of hands. They did not know how it all happened, but that is what they had seen occur in other countries. Why not here? Fair's fair. But the group around the table had more pressing concerns... Would they have their SEL in black or navy blue?

'You are here to build the hotel,' I was told.

'No, I am here to look for a *possible* site. Someone else has to fund and build it. We could design and run it.'

The meeting droned on, lecturing me on the importance of hosting this OAU meeting while the remains of the Mercedes brochure were pawed to death. The deputy secretary to the Assistant Minister of Tourism (you get a lot of job creation where there is 90+% unemployment) mentioned the beauty of the offshore islands which were claimed to be unspoilt and World Class. They were the inspiration for 'Treasure Island', I was told. They would delight any Western tourists. This sounded slightly more promising. I asked when I could see them.

'Immediately.'

'Immediately? Let's go.'

Then he started counting off on his fingers, one day to apply for the permit to use the Government Boat. (Apply for a permit to apply for...?) Then you could apply for a permit for the fuel, then...

When he reached the fingers on his other hand I cut in.

'We are talking about a week here, aren't we?'

He flashed a Steinway grin. 'Yes, Sah. Immediately.'

I am not saying that all West African Government officials are lazy, racist, greedy, nose-picking crooks.

Just the ones I have met.

It was actually the next day that I found myself at a crumbling set of harbour steps awaiting the Government Boat. It was obvious that strings or jungle vines had been pulled to compress this massive chain of bureaucratic events into a mere 24 hours.

The harbour looked like D-Day plus 3. Wrecked hulks and masts poked up at crazy angles through the surface scum. Oil and debris floated on the water. It smelt like Saltley gas works and looked like the top of an effluence tank. Nearly all the drowned vessels had rusted weapons attached and bristled with massive aerials.

'The Russians gave us these trawlers,' explained my minder. 'But they started leaking. They did not come back to fix them.'

My 'Why didn't you fix them?' was met with disbelief that such a stupid question should be dignified with an answer.

I asked if there were any privately owned boats, was there a yacht club? Can we get lunch there? No. Not since The Imperialists left. You are not allowed to own a boat unless you are a citizen of the country.

So if I became a citizen here, could I own a boat?

'No. You have to be a citizen of *indigenous descent.*'

'So I have to be black to own a boat here?'

'Yes.'

So that rules out Michael Jackson and me, even if we had a subscription to *The Guardian*... A brand new 11 foot inflatable and a fresh out of the box outboard showed up at the steps with three officials dressed in the rig of their heroes, Ton ton Macouts, in suits and sinister sunnies.

My minder and I climbed in (are you counting? That's five in an 11 foot inflatable). I mentally added a pair of trousers to my expense claim and we dodged out through the wrecks. Eventually we could see the offshore islands beyond the harbour mouth. Do you remember seeing pictures of how they chop up old ships on the beaches in India and Bangladesh? They were like that. Just littered with wrecks and debris. But nobody was cutting them up.

'Where is the Government boat kept?' I asked as we began to head out of the harbour. I had expected we were being ferried to a harbour launch that would be used for this offshore passage, but no, this inflatable was it... I told them to turn around, carefully, I had seen enough.

My flight was that night, from an airport with only three working fluorescent tubes. The departure tax from this Tourist's Delight was the snatched contents of my wallet. With the same gratitude as when Charles Laughton's Hunchback claimed sanctuary when he tottered into Notre Dame Cathedral, I reached the air conditioned sanctuary of the door to the airliner which would be returning me to the outside world and all that it contained... Elected governments, Council regulations, public utilities, drains, a free and critical press, Greenies and languages containing that unknown word in the developing world – 'maintenance'.

My minder was on the tarmac below and shouted up.

'When will you start building the hotel?'

'Immediately.'

Is this the yacht club?

Welcome to Australia

Quirkie becomes an unwitting criminal accomplice to his new-found friend

David does not come across as your average Zambian. He speaks in fluent French, Italian, German, Danish, ChiBemba and Cockney. He writes songs and poetry that brings tears to your heart. (He gave away a bunch of songs in a pub one night in exchange for a round of drinks. One of them wound up on the back of *Streets of London*, which seemed to be in the top ten forever.) He ran a restaurant where he cooked for Elizabeth Taylor and Prince Charles (no, they were not together). He skippered ocean racing yachts and his own trawler. He can fix any mechanical problem that would defeat British Aerospace and the Williams Racing Team. He had made and lost a fortune on the Stock Exchange and had surprised his doctors by surviving a coma and life threatening injuries received from a drunk driver. He is of lightweight construction, carries scars and a slight stoop from his injuries and is pale pink in colour.

When I first met David, he was standing on the mainland jetty wearing battered sneakers, crutch-cutting, paint-stained shorts from primary school, a torn T-shirt with pigs doing rude things to each other and squinty narrow sunglasses. He carried most of his worldly possessions over one shoulder, a patched-to-death knapsack and a guitar in a fibreglass case. He had a can of Fosters in one hand and a matchstick thin roll-up in the other. At the time, he did not present himself as being one of the cleverest and most talented people I've ever met.

We had also newly arrived in Australia and were enjoying the Christmas Holiday at his sister's beach house. There was no land access, so David was being collected by ferry. He had backpacked across half the world and was taking a break before tackling the other bit.

At the beach house, David found this dependence on the ferry as our only link the mainland, a little onerous. He said we needed a boat of our own. The next morning he caught the first ferry out, saying he would be looking for a boat.

At the end of the day, there was no sign of David and I was about to open the first 'Sundowner' when a cry came from offshore. David was approaching, sitting astride the foredeck of a battered fibreglass outboard runabout, paddling with an old fence paling. I helped him drag it ashore.

'We got a boat,' he grinned, and grabbed my beer.

The next day, with only the tools from the boot of his sister's second hand car, he stripped the engine on the beach.

'Just needs a bit of a clean out,' he said. 'Bloke tried to launch this at the ramp. No bungs in the boat. Didn't have his car in gear, pulled it into the drink, had to disconnect the trailer to get the car pulled out. The boat sank. It'd been underwater for two tides when I met him. He was so teed off with it. I acquired it for a trifling amount.'

'How trifling?'

'His wife said she did not want to set eyes on the thing again, said he could never get it to work and if he thought he was planning to bring that home with them, she would not be there. I gave him a slab of beer for it...'

The outboard motor was about 30 hp but of a make quite unknown to me.

'These are a pretty naff engine,' he explained. 'American, but still junk. Maybe alright on the Midwestern lakes, freshwater and plenty of local dealers. Still... cheap at half the price.'

Half way into the afternoon, the peace was shredded by the snarl of an engine and clouds of blue smoke. With only the most basic of tools, no instruction manual and on a diet of roll-ups, beer and his sister's sloppy beetroot sandwiches, David had effortlessly achieved a nonchalant mechanical miracle.

'Right,' he grinned. 'Let's take the kids for a spin.'

And so he did. The rest of the day was full of spray and howls of delight as David thrilled every child on the beach with wild rides in the Slabcraft, as he called it.

'Here, this thing's running alright, isn't it? We should be able to pull water skiers with it.'

The following morning saw Uncle David Pied Pipering the children on a beachcombing expedition. They found another driftwood fence paling to match his paddle, and under the house what had to be a pre-war saw. The kids gathered armloads of bits of rope and string. The skis were elegantly crafted from the palings with wedged fronts nailed on. Your feet went into two anonymous sneakers of almost similar size. These had been wired to the palings and wire through the lace holes secured the sneakers to a variety of foot sizes.

'Right, Quirkie, you first. We need a volunteer to see how safe these things are.' I wired the 'quick release' sneakers to my feet, grabbed the piece of branch tied to a medley of string and rope that was our ski line while David again demonstrated he was the only one who could start this engine. The Slabcraft heaved itself onto the plane and to my astonishment I was up and skimming behind it on the two fence palings.

David was either demonstrating the manoeuvring ability of the boat or trying to dump me when we noticed we were being paced by another boat. It had men in uniforms aboard and NSW Marine Services Board water police on the side. David stopped the boat and turned off the motor. I unwired the skis and paddled down to hear the ensuing exchange.

Old sneakers drilled and wired
to skis. Note quick release
wire laces...

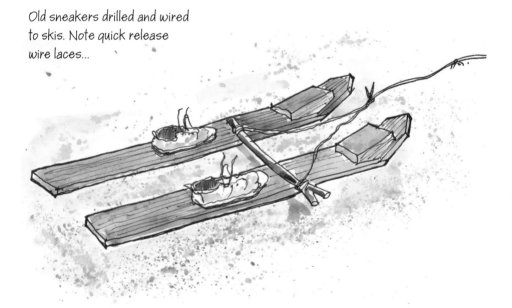

'Registration papers?' asked David. 'What are they? No, I picked this up a couple days ago from a bloke at the ramp. His name and address? No idea, he drove a beige Holden. Manual. The back half is very wet. Had a wife with red hair. I think she was a Cheryl. Might have been Kylie. A Boating Licence? What are they? Need those for boats doing more than 10 knots, do you? Well, I did not know that. An observer for water skiing? Yes, well, we were not sure that we had enough power to get one up on skis so we did not want the extra weight aboard, so one of the kids? No? Have to be over 16, do they? And water ski lines have to be 18 metres? Sorry, this is all the string we could find...'

The litany of offences and indiscretions mounted and the officer turned the pages of his notebook. David explained how he acquired the drowned boat and engine and got it working and then made the skiing gear from debris. The officer looked at me for confirmation and noticing the paling skis with sneakers floating on the water.

He shook his head and said the reason they came to inspect us was that we did not have an observer but he also recognised the make of engine and this was the first time he had seen one running smoothly and pulling a skier. Only then did our other legal transgressions become obvious.

'Yeah, bit of a dodgy motor aren't they?' agreed David and he gave technical details of how he had given it the kiss of life to the two fascinated water police.

'Dodgy?' said the officer ripping up the list of our criminal activity. Let me tell you how dodgy they are, I have been in the water police for over 20 years now and not one of these engines, not one, has ever been reported stolen.' He grinned and reached over and shook David's hand. 'Welcome to Australia, mate. This country needs people like you. Get an observer in the boat and have a great day.'

BACK TO THE STONE AGE

Quirkie takes a step back in time, with surprising results

The Malabar Coast. Say it to yourself. Swill those words around in your mouth. Taste good, don't they? Like those languid cadenzas in John Masefield's *Cargoes* before the dirty British Coaster butts in.

The Malabar Coast is the South Western shore of Kerala, the Southernmost Indian State. It is a string of lagoons flung along the country's South Western tip. I flew in there to inspect

"Can you get that garboard strake sewn up before my annual survey?"

possible hotel sites among the lagoons. When we boarded that domestic Indian airliner at Madras, now Chennai, we were all herded up the rear stairs. On landing, all the other passengers stood up and I noticed that I was the only who was not talking on a mobile phone. I did not own one at the time. However, I was possibly the only passenger who appeared to own a pair of socks. To exit, those up front could use the foreward stairs, which gave disturbing views of the car body filler which had been used to patch the leading edge of the port wing. I am not kidding here.

I was collected by a placard waving duo and escorted to an Ambassador car, a locally built version of the 1950s Morris *Oxford* but without the fine finish and the exhilarating performance. Particularly this one. Our journey was 88 miles by the odometer and 4½ hours by my watch. 19½ mph due to traffic conditions, rutted dirt roads, cow jams and the puny Isuzu diesel engine which did not have the strength to power an electric toothbrush. The Lynmouth to Porlock Lifeboat crew could have pulled us faster.

At a landing stage by one of the lagoons, we were met by the Indian Architect who had been our partner there for 15 years and was acting as guide and interpreter. There were a few mud and tin shack dukas in a clearing. I pointed out why this shopping centre had something that had not been seen in my old neighbourhood for a generation; all the signs were in English.

My guide explained, 'It is a National Law here that all shop signage must be in Official Language of the Country; English.' Now there's an original thought... Why hasn't the readership of *The Guardian* condemned this Indian regulation as racist?

The local boats were interesting; canoes about 20 feet long, each one was stitched together from firewood rejects with vegetable fibre and some black sticky stuff in the seams. My guide explained that these were traditional craft dating back thousands of years to before the availability of metal fastenings. *Before* metal fastenings? That was the Stone Age. Even the Vikings ditched sewing for metal fastenings when somebody discovered iron and opened a chandlery. But these people are too poor to afford metal, said our partner.

Our voyage to the site was to be in a couple of these Biblical craft. The boatmen looked like shrink-wrapped skeletons. They were fuse-wire thin and had the polished black complexion of Nubian tribesmen with dazzlingly perfect grins no toothpaste commercial could ever match. They each wore a

The de luxe model came with aux. sail. This one has a cargo of portable housing...

curiously bulky dhoti or loin cloth. The canoes were poled through the shallow waterways at walking pace.

We were on our way back from the site when the heavens opened. Rain hammered down and the surface of the lagoon sprouted white grass. A millisecond before the downpour started, our stone age mariners had a quick fumble in their dhotis and with the precision of Duo of Radio City Rockets, each swept out a folding umbrella! These were opened and tucked beneath an armpit with barely a slowing of the stroke.

While these boatmen were perfectly dry, Indiana Quirk here sat in the stern, soaked and frozen, using half a calabash gourd to bail, trying to keep my faithful safari boots above water.

Above the roar of the water I heard an improbable sound. Maybe they have some form of tropical bird here that sounds like that but no, our skipper, who could not afford metal fastenings, had another quick fumble and clapped his hand to his ear. On this primitive, sewn together relic of Old Testament days, he had just taken a call on his mobile phone...

THE MOON AND 2½P

Quirkie recalls how he encountered an idyllic tropical lifestyle, which seemed reminiscent of an updated Somerset Maugham story

Whenever some pontificating Know All dredges up a hackneyed cliché like 'you can't have it all', I politely let them have their say then gently belt them between the eyes with the parable of the cheese, the luggage and the bomb scare. Please feel free to do the same.

A bunch of us had accepted the invitation from an old Aussie mate to join him in New Guinea and waft westwards aboard his motor sailer. No sooner had we bribed our first official to clear port, when our old Sheila-chasing, hard drinking carnivore of a skipper announced that he had become an abstemious celibate vegan. The ship's stores reflected this. Our Aussie aid gifts of cheese, cheer and frozen meat had been left ashore as he planned to introduce us to the joys of his new lifestyle.

Two weeks later, we anchored near a drop dead gorgeous 60 foot ketch moored outside a new gold plated resort. It was a magical setting all illuminated by a romantic half moon blazing

away on its back like a Chernobyl toenail clipping. We left the skipper to continue his love affair with veggie juice and lentils while we rowed ashore looking for the coldest beer in the southern hemisphere. The hotel lobby bar opened onto a vista of a magical palm fringed shoreline with the ketch as a centre piece. The whole hotel was perfection in tropical hospitality design, blighted by one thing. A little heap of acne and sneakers, illuminated by the bilious blue glow of a laptop screen. (And yes, it has a baseball cap on backwards.) These laptops should be checked at the counter, like six shooters in a Dodge City saloon. Is it only Americans that do this? The Aussies are all at the bar, the Germans are planning a Panzer attack on the buffet and the Poms are off complaining about

Why don't these things come with instructions?

He was playing a card game

Americans call these 'shorts'

I used to have a dinghy that was smaller than these

something. A feigned stumble by our largest crew member and a bit of spilt beer brought most satisfactory results.

There was a squeak from Noo Joisey adenoids.

'Claim it on your travel insurance, *when you get back.*' Advised our crewman.

After the restorative powers of a few swift beers, we hit the dining room with the etiquette of a bunch of lab rats let loose in Harrods's food hall.

'So you like your cheese?' enquired a crisply rigged thirty something Kiwi as the staff struggled to reload the buffet with what is an expensive luxury in Asia. We explained that we were on a famine relief project. Ours. He sympathised with our explanation and introduced himself as Steve. We introduced him to a vacant seat.

Steve had obviously been away from Nuh Z'luhnd for a while and mixing with Aussies and Poms as his diction was showing the first green shoots of vowels. These are quite rare in spoken Kiwi.

He had been Food & Beverage Manager for an International hotel group before taking time out to work on a classic sailing charter yacht in South East Asia. It was a perfect lifestyle but a part of his conscience and many letters from his Mum made him concerned about easing back into his career. He set up some interviews in Europe, took a week off, and bought some sharp suits and a bucket shop airline ticket. To show he wasn't a boat-bumming Kiwi, he spent a fortune on a top of the line imported suit carrier.

After a freezing, slush encrusted week of interviews, airports and traffic, he questioned if he really wanted to get back into this collar and tie lifestyle. To cheer himself up, he loaded his Louis Vuitton suit carrier with the finest cheeses that Europe could offer.

'We were over India when the bomb scare was announced,' said Steve. 'We landed at some remote airport where there bomb disposal technique was to spread the entire luggage out at the far side of the airport. If nothing went bang by the end of the day, they put it all back in the plane and took off. I spent a 40 degree day in a tin shed watching my luggage melt. Then we were off again.'

Any readers old enough to have cleaned a fondue fork will sympathise with Steve's dilemma. The whole congealed mess, suits, shirts and everything that represented a corporate career was given a naval funeral in the South China Sea.

'I remember it all seemed very significant at the time,' recalled Steve.

That evening the charter yacht was joined by an even grander one and Steve entertained the guests with his traveller's tale. A middle aged American from the other yacht didn't laugh. 'He asked me to go through the obituary list of the cheese I bought. I could swear there were tears in his eyes. The next morning, he offered me a job. He wanted someone with an F&B background who knew the area to help him open a chain of boutique resorts he was planning.

'This is the eighth I have opened for him.'

When he wasn't living in a six star resort, signing chits for everything, Steve had to rough it aboard his 60 foot ketch, which now graced the hotel's anchorage, being preened to perfection by its white uniformed crew.

'Life can be strange at times,' reflected Steve, returning the smiles of two grain-fed mid-Western girls while eyeing his ketch and obviously doing calculations in his head. 'If it hadn't been for a few quids' worth of cheese, the bomb scare and the way they handled it, I could be in a raincoat, waiting for a bus at Gatwick now. Mind you, I would have a very nice suit carrier.'

Pontoon Anyone?

Quirkie is asked to extend a holiday house which has a few problems, and begins a long association with the local hospital

Neighbour's boathouse (bigger!)

Hinged gangway accommodates 2M tidal range 11'6" clanker ply skiff we built for access across the creek

When I first met the client who would later become my landlady, I thought she was a Pom. She could say the word 'No' in one syllable. (And she did this a lot.) Most Aussie Sheilas say it the same way as the bloke who built the ark. This is how my landlady bought a holiday house. While slurping through a rainy lunch at a friend's place on Patonga creek, the sun suddenly came out and the world looked beautiful.

Hard has kept the same pair of Ray Bans for 40 years. Pimms No 5. You could power a spitfire on the ones he makes.

to
se

'How wonderful! I would love a place like this when I have finished in my tour in Hong Kong. Anything for sale?' A quick stroll along the other 40 odd houses showed nothing of interest.

'I like the house next door but one, do you have the owner's number? Thanks.'

'Hello, you don't know me but I am having lunch with Dain and Alyson, your neighbours,

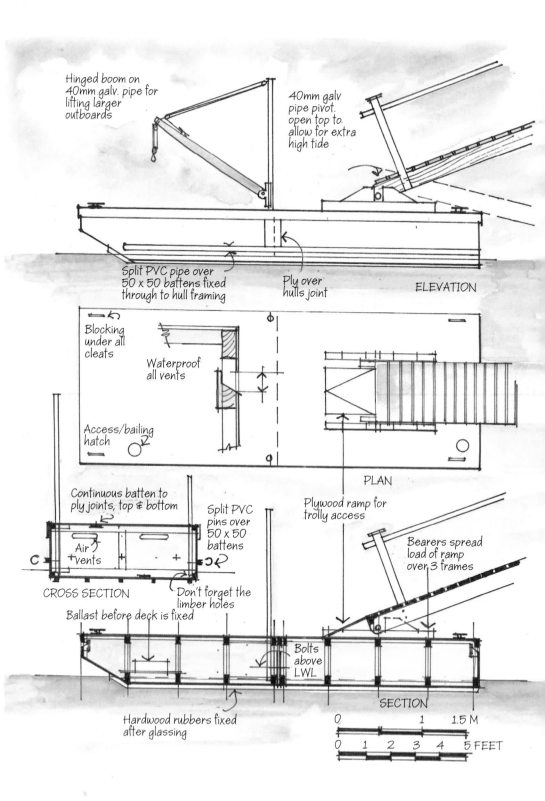

Hinged boom on 40mm galv. pipe for lifting larger outboards

40mm galv pipe pivot. open top to allow for extra high tide

Split PVC pipe over 50 x 50 battens fixed through to hull framing

Ply over hulls joint

ELEVATION

Blocking under all cleats

Waterproof all vents

Access/bailing hatch

PLAN

Continuous batten to ply joints, top & bottom

Split PVC pins over 50 x 50 battens

Air vents

CROSS SECTION

Don't forget the limber holes

Ballast before deck is fixed

Hardwood rubbers fixed after glassing

Plywood ramp for trolly access

Bearers spread load of ramp over 3 frames

Bolts above LWL

SECTION

0   1   1.5 M

0   1   2   3   4   5 FEET

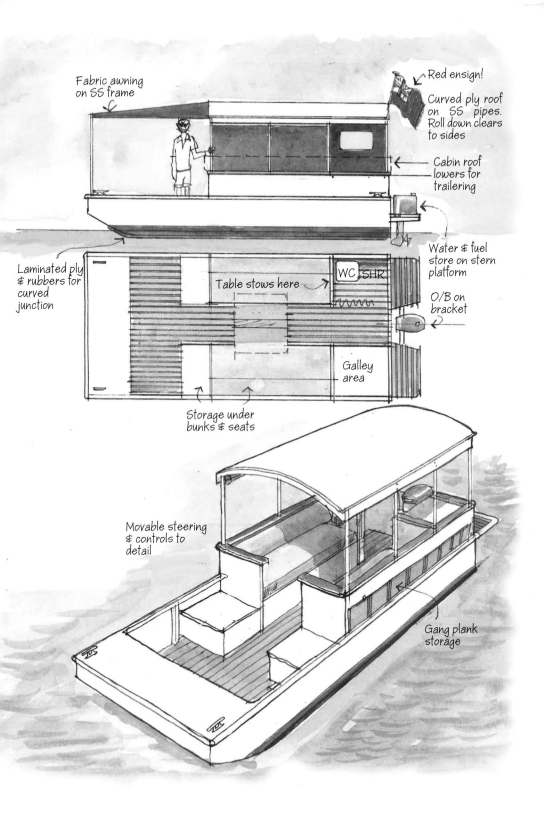

Fabric awning
on SS frame

Red ensign!

Curved ply roof
on SS pipes.
Roll down clears
to sides

Cabin roof
lowers for
trailering

Water & fuel
store on stern
platform

O/B on
bracket

Laminated ply
& rubbers for
curved
junction

Table stows here

WC SHR

Galley
area

Storage under
bunks & seats

Movable steering
& controls to
detail

Gang plank
storage

yes, lovely people, aren't they? I was wondering if ever you thought of selling... Really. You had it valued last week?' And before climbing into dessert, they had a deal.

A post-purchase inspection revealed loads of potential and few shortcomings. Like having no land access, nor drainage and BYO rainwater for a water supply. I was asked to design the extensions and renovations and that's where the problems really started. No builder would look at it.

So eventually I nibbled at the work myself over a few years with a batch of skilled and entertaining back packers. But first, how do we get the building materials over the 100m wide tidal creek? It was quite shallow in places. Tom Cruise could wade across it at low water and not get his teeth wet.

Tom Cruise wouldn't get his teeth wet. . .

I recalled the wartime British Army 20 foot plywood pontoons and sketched up something similar, 16 x 6 x 2 foot and had the materials for this delivered to the house site aboard the local oyster punt. I had the use of a neighbour's boathouse for three days before he started his next project. By mass producing the frames, one over another and with the occasional help of a transient drunk, we had the pontoon built, glassed all over and launched in three days. That included trying to lift it, realising we couldn't, dropping it, getting across the creek to have my toenail removed at the local hospital, making life-long friends there, limping back, cutting the pontoon into two, adding two new transoms, glassing again, then painting it, chucking the bits into the creek and bolting them together.

It carried up to two and a half tons when lashed to an eleven foot tinny with my 20 year old 4 hp Evenrude. It only sank once, and now serves as a floating pontoon at the end of the 70 foot jetty. It may be of interest to someone who faces an aquatic transport problem or needs a similar floating structure. However, I wish I had thought about the afterlife, some of the other uses for which the pontoon could have been put, as was pointed out recently.

An overseas visitor made some interesting comments.

I have known Howard (pronounced 'Hard') for over 40 years. As well as being an active and keen sailor, he has been flying for longer than that and still in his original Ray Bans... Seeing Africa from 'God's Eye' as Karen Blixen wrote, can be spectacular, but tedious. Your tiny plane crawls over the vast hide of Africa like an insect across an elephant's back. But in Hard's handkerchief fabric covered two seater you always felt World War 2 was still going, you had to keep an eye out for the Hun in the Sun. Dive bombing friends' houses and cars or anything of interest was always part of the mission. It was with him over the Ngong Hills that to escape a possible squadron of ME 109's lurking in a batch of cumulous that my curry lunch and I first looped the loop. Separately.

Anyway, he speaks in the clipped extreme Anglo shorthand that reminds you of a mix between one of those RAF types from morale boosting wartime films, Biggles and Bertie Wooster. All of whom, you thought, had been extinct. He is single-handedly keeping the British cravat industry afloat.

He paced out the pontoon deck throwing out ideas. This is him speaking:

'I say, chum, dash it all, your pontoon has given me an idea. Three days to build you say? Hmmm. How would it be if you made one as a sort of trailerable houseboat? I mean, a bit of a forward cockpit, you know, then a couple of settee bunks and you could get a bit of a galley and a cho (Swahili for 'dunny') even a sun shower right aft here. Put your jolly old outboard on a pod, keep it out of the boat. Rig up a folding lid that gives you full headroom, some roll down clears and it all comes down flat when you heave the whole thing on your trailer. Tow it over the Channel and you're off down the Canals of Europe. Living on cheese and wine. I say, can you catch scurvy like that? Of course the confounded EU regulations might sink you with bureaucracy but a damned attractive proposition, what? Got to be a way around stupid regulations. Make it a prototype. Might put the beam up from six to eight feet, the max for towing, unless you wanted to explore the UK canals and play Colonel Fawcett discovering Wigan pier and scraping though those ridiculous seven foot locks. No, forget it. Brain must be overheating. Go for eight feet. Then right through France to the Med. Red ensign flying all the way. Glorious. Fancy another Pimms?'

And it wouldn't be hard, would it? Using a lighter construction than I did (and safety boots) it would be quick, cheap and easy. One of the Creekie neighbours regularly uses their trailer sailer to explore different reaches of the Murray each year. An interesting design exercise.

I have to be polite to 'Hard' these days. He is the father in law of one of my lofty lads... and now answers to the name of Hobbit. And we are both grandfathers to the same lovely granddaughter. Maybe we should both take her through the French canals when she is older...

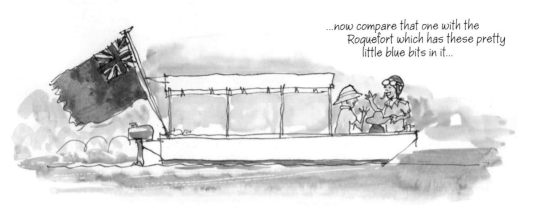

...now compare that one with the Roquefort which has these pretty little blue bits in it...

Hard and Quirkie take their granddaughter on an educational cruise through France

'IF YOU WANT TO GET AHEAD...

Quirkie, the fashion Guru of Patonga Creek, reflects on perhaps why he didn't

...get a hat' said the old ad, when grown ups wore trilbies and tried to look like Humphrey Bogart. At that time, half a century ago, there were perhaps three accepted types of nautical headgear.

1) The woolly cap, pom pom optional. Gave you a bad hair day for the rest of your life.
2) The floppy sunhat. For the eternal optimist (why else would you own a boat?). Apparently, sales slumped when Gilligan bumbled across our TV screens wearing this and the same red shirt for 98 episodes.
3) The full blown Yachting Cap. At the top end of the scale. A formal Navy inspired creation, ideal for messing about in everyday boating events such as having your photograph taken for a book you had just written, accepting the surrender of the German North Sea Fleet or even getting invited to one of those summits on navigation lights with the editor of *Yachting World*.

Pom pom optional

Our skipper, Jack, gave that impression, at least from a distance, with a cast-off cap from an Odeon doorman and a white plastic cover from the Army and Navy Disposal store. ('Sorry sir, just the covers. No caps.')

Sir F Chichester suddenly made wearing modified baseball caps acceptable on circumnavigations. It was no longer mandated that you wear these things with Day Glow T-shirts, Bermooda Shorts, white wall sneakers and an ice cream.

The Mountbatten flavoured cap faded as we all wanted to look cool in those Greek Fishermen's caps under which Greek Fishermen sweated under a Mediterranean sun. But they looked really cool while doing it.

I find this passion to look like real sailors rather curious when the last real sailors of my generation – leather featured old salts who edged those remaining trading ketches and schooners around West Country headlands – wore an Oxfam blend of hard black shoes or boots, grey flannels, and a hand knitted Guernsey topped off with a fag and a tweed cap. They just didn't look the part. Certainly not to people who buy cans of paint with pictures of boats on them.

Cool Greek chic

In foul weather, nothing beats a Sou'wester. Not only do you look as nautical as the old salt on a tin of Skipper's Sardines, but secured under the chin you are just about bombproof.

As nautical as the old salt on a tin of Skipper's sardines

No, he's just testing the wind with a wet finger.

The last real sailors

My personal boating choice is a hat rack full of almost disposable baseball caps, although they are all rigged with lanyards and a safety pin to moor them to the collar of a T-shirt. (I used to tie them to the label, but my entire wardrobe comes from Asian street vendors so the labels have been macheted out.)

Apart from the Panama hat, which is actually made down the road in Equator, there is one piece of warm weather headgear which has been sadly neglected of late. I speak of course of the pith helmet or Bombay Bowler, a sort of tropical Sou'wester. Mine was 50 years out of date when I acquired it 40 years ago. They make forgeries in Vietnam, but without the essential leather supporting band. Also, they have funny shaped heads there, or perhaps they use a rugger ball as a mould. Sideways. Under an Equatorial sun, the helmet can shade your shoulders and its cork insulated crown is suspended via the leather sweatband above the head, thus allowing a cooling air flow which prevents the brain from overheating.

Apart from a slight lifting tendency in winds over Force 3, I see only one problem. You look a proper pratt wearing it...

Note: generous shade area protects wearer and Pimms

Queen of the Creek

Or: 20 things some bastard ought to have told me before I started building this bloody thing. Quirkie has been in love for 25 years. It's time to consummate the deal

It has been said that if you plan to build a boat, first build the dinghy. Some of my more seagoing neighbours were understandably concerned when I started building, at home, the dinghy for the 100 foot schooner *America*.

I had been captivated by Pete Culler's design for the yawl boats he designed and built for the 1967 replica of *America* in his glorious book *Skiffs and Schooners*. My copy would fall open at pages 90–91, where Pete had generously provided the lines and offsets. For a quarter of a century I had treasured this book and reckoned the yawl had to be one of the finest looking boats of her length ever created, but the detailed craftsmanship and finishing required for such a gem would be far beyond my ability to build. This would be yacht building, not just boat building. Just look at the challenge of those black topsides, for example. They would have to be mirror smooth. Any imperfections would show up like cellulite on a starlet's thighs.

It's odd how unrelated events can push us into a course of action. One Friday lunchtime I flicked through a newsagent's copy of a local boat magazine that featured a string of God-awful clunkers, all amateur designed and built, all full of corners and painted in colours you would not inflict on a chook shed. Was this to be the future of amateur boat building?

Later that afternoon, I heard that the recently widowed owner of the house in which I was living and acting as house sitter and personal servant to an eccentric cat, would be remaining overseas for another two years... Two years? That should be long enough...

That evening I measured the space under the first floor balcony. It had full crouching headroom and there would be nearly five and a half inches' clearance between the columns and either side of the gunwales of the yawl's five foot beam. Not wishing to repeat my father's mistake when he built a copy of a William Lyons Swallow Sports sidecar (which became SS, then Jaguar) in the basement, I carefully measured the exit route of the finished boat. It would have to be turned sideways and would involve being caesareaned through the neighbour's hedge. How could he refuse? His name is Rudder and his dad was a boat builder.

So I fired up the photocopier and next morning kicked a roll of brown wrapping paper across the deck. Three years later, we launched the *Queen of the Creek* and she is a joy to behold, spears through the water under the waft of a single oar and turns heads like a movie star.

My world changed a lot during the time I nibbled away at building her. I started with limited skills and the house owner's late husband's tools and acquired a few of my own as work progressed. I learned a lot during construction. Here are some of the things I wish I had known before starting.

1. Workshopmanship

As a lifelong natural born slob, it really grieves me to lead off with this, but tidiness counts. If all your tools don't have a home to go to, you can waste the best years of your life looking for things as trivial as a drill bit. Pencils are the worst. They will escape from your pocket and hide under a pile of distant wood shavings. I think they are related to socks in washing machines. A builder's belt helps for some of the smaller tools; hammer, pencils, tape measures, squares, pliers etc. These belts can look quite good on the right helper. In the interests of World Peace, get your own vacuum cleaner for the boat and workshop.

2. Time and costs
I can tell you that from rolling out the lofting paper until the last of the 92 planks were installed took 59.5 hours. But from there to completion I could only guess that it took twice as long. So keep an accurate log of time and costs right throughout the job.

3. Lofting counts
Lofting is not really a black art, just don't get lost while you are doing it. While lofting the ferro-schooner in a previous life I hit on the idea of using different colours for each waterline, buttock and station. You don't need many, just enough to avoid confusion with its neighbour. And if you write the dimension on each set out point, it further reduces the confusion.

For fairing battens, I used lengths of the cedar strip planking taped together and sprung them between thin finishing nails driven into the set out points. To transfer the dimensions from the lines to the body plan, I found it easier and more accurate to use scrap paper tick strips than measuring each item with a ruler or tape.

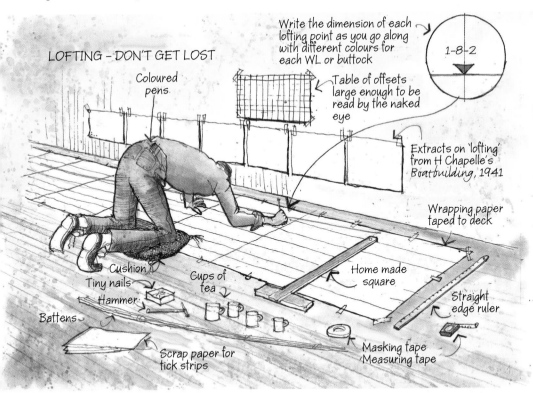

LOFTING – DON'T GET LOST

Write the dimension of each lofting point as you go along with different colours for each WL or buttock

1-8-2

Coloured pens

Table of offsets large enough to be read by the naked eye

Extracts on 'lofting' from H Chapelle's *Boatbuilding*, 1941

Wrapping paper taped to deck

Cushion
Tiny nails
Hammer
Battens

Cups of tea

Home made square

Straight edge ruler

Scrap paper for tick strips

Masking tape
Measuring tape

4. The mouldy bit
OK, so you have the lines lofted... now what? How do you get them onto the building material? I have heard of the ritual dance that some professional boat builders do after placing a series of nails around the lines and laying the mould material on top. However, I bought some A1 sized tracing paper and traced the half moulds, their waterlines and buttocks, with a 2B pencil.

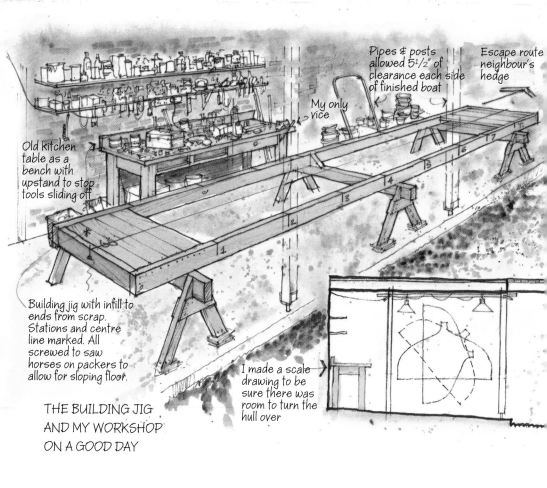

Pipes & posts allowed 5½" of clearance each side of finished boat

Escape route neighbour's hedge

My only vice

Old kitchen table as a bench with upstand to stop tools sliding off

Building jig with infill to ends from scrap. Stations and centre line marked. All screwed to saw horses on packers to allow for sloping floor.

I made a scale drawing to be sure there was room to turn the hull over

THE BUILDING JIG
AND MY WORKSHOP
ON A GOOD DAY

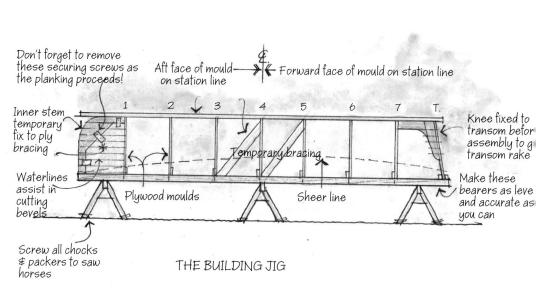

Don't forget to remove these securing screws as the planking proceeds!

Aft face of mould on station line

Forward face of mould on station line

Inner stem temporary fix to ply bracing

Knee fixed to transom befor assembly to g transom rake

Waterlines assist in cutting bevels

Temporary bracing

Plywood moulds

Sheer line

Make these bearers as leve and accurate as you can

Screw all chocks & packers to saw horses

THE BUILDING JIG

The sheet is turned over and laid on the mould matrial and you accurately trace each line again. This transfers the original lead markings onto the mould. Now flip it over and transfer the other half... I scrounged a batch of old 20mm plywood flooring panels for the moulds and found it quite economical as you can mark one above the other like a two dimensional version of the old wooden dolls.

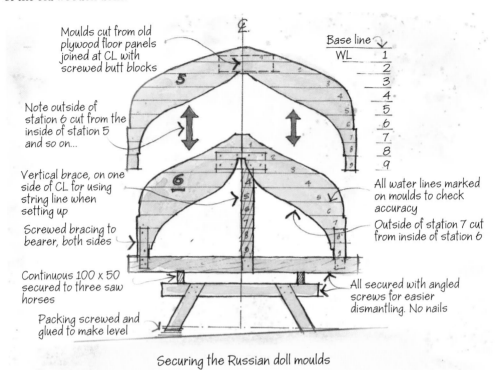

Moulds cut from old plywood floor panels joined at CL with screwed butt blocks

Note outside of station 6 cut from the inside of station 5 and so on...

Vertical brace, on one side of CL for using string line when setting up

Screwed bracing to bearer, both sides

Continuous 100 x 50 secured to three saw horses

Packing screwed and glued to make level

Base line
WL

All water lines marked on moulds to check accuracy

Outside of station 7 cut from inside of station 6

All secured with angled screws for easier dismantling. No nails

Securing the Russian doll moulds

5. Strip planking

I would now never consider building a strip plank boat without using an interlocking tongue and groove type. It is so much easier to use; you can just whizz the glue into the groove and pop it into the waiting tongue of the previous plank. I did everything single-handed with full length planks and did not break one, but if I had, the T&G mouldings hold broken or scarfed planks together and perfectly aligned. I started off with three strips of 65 x 8 mm strips starting from the gunwale but had to change to 15 x 8 mm for the rest of the hull in order to handle the dreaded bends and twists as shown on the sketch.

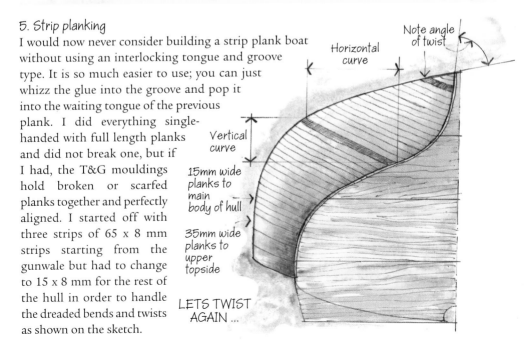

Note angle of twist

Horizontal curve

Vertical curve

15mm wide planks to main body of hull

35mm wide planks to upper topside

LETS TWIST AGAIN ...

There are ways to minimise the strips and wastage by starting the strips at the top and the bottom, then trimming the ones in between. But this means not every plank can be full length. To me, this was not an option.

6. Glues

I did not use epoxy to join the strips, only to secure the plank ends to the stem and transom. Not only is epoxy a pain to mix and thicken, but more importantly it's a killer on tools when smoothing the hull. I used Purbond, a brilliant Oz-made single pack polyurethane glue which foams up if you dampen the timber and fills any gaps. It resembles honeycomb when it dries and I trimmed off the dribbles when dry with an old bread knife. As the planks were only 15mm wide, there was minimum finishing with the hand plane. But you should wear gloves when using this glue as contact with it gives you one week's membership of the Black Hand Gang.

7. Dracularisation

Anyone living in Wolverhampton or further north can skip the next paragraph. While fibreglassing the upturned hull, a ray of Aussie sunlight sneaked into my stygian workshop with dramatic effects on a plastic container of epoxy hardener. It was turned into a bubbling, frothing weapon of mass destruction. I instinctively grabbed it. Not a good idea. The melting container stuck to my fingers. I managed to fling it onto a cool area of shaded concrete where it finally died like Christopher Lee used to do at the end of those old Hammer Horror films. Lesson learned: do not leave any of your epoxy out in the sun.

8. Screws

There are maybe about a dozen or so metal fastenings in the finished boat, to secure the knees. Everything else is epoxy-jointed using temporary screws and clamps to hold everything together.

To avoid the screws from sticking to the amazing epoxy, first I marinated them in liquid soap. Don't use the otherwise excellent plasterboard screws for narrow strip plank construction. The countersunk head splays the soft timber.

Counter sunk screw heads crush cedar strips and widen the plank at the joint, resulting in gaps . . .

Use furniture screws, which come with a built-in washer, you won't need many, as soon as the glue on the first batch of strips has set, you can take them out and use them on the next lot. By the way, you would think that stainless steel screws would be stronger than the regular hardware store/plasterboard variety, wouldn't

. . .so use pan headed screws with a washer or furniture screws which are born like this.

you? So did I, but this is not the case. You need to be really gentle with them and only use them where you need the belt and braces security of epoxy and metal fastenings.

That's why I now favour using dowelling to hold bits together, as I did with four layers of Jarrah for the keel. You might need a bit of clamping pressure until the glue sets, but you can smooth it afterwards without worrying that you have left a screw behind, which will show up as a nick in your plane blade.

9. Use protection

Don't let your favourite drill anywhere near the boat while you are planking up. The glue gets everywhere. I have heard of dedicated builders who dress their drills in breathable cloth bags, but it's probably better to buy one of these 'on special' variable speed bargain drills at your local hardware store. You won't be putting a great deal of load on it, just glue. Just be sure you finish the boat before the warranty expires.

10. Laminating v Steaming

I found it easier to build up pieces like the stem and later the gunwales by laminating rather that steaming. I recycled some old Jarrah floorboards to make an icebreaker stem. You use an adjustable square to take the bevels from your lofting plan and transfer these to the stem. While planing

Always use protection...

this really tough West Australian hardwood, I spared a thought for those craftsmen who had whittled HMS *Victory* out of 2,000 Oak trees, using soft iron tools of the period...

I once built a model of a clinker dinghy from cardboard, only about 5 inches long. What was astonishing was the additional stiffness when I glued in minute ribs from slivers of postcard. I wanted the *Queen* to have the traditional look of ribs so that she would not be mistaken for

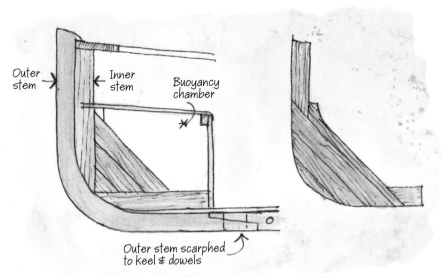

BUILDING UP THE INNER STEM
Two layers of Jarrah floorboard offcuts, with staggered joints, glued together.
Outer stem similar.

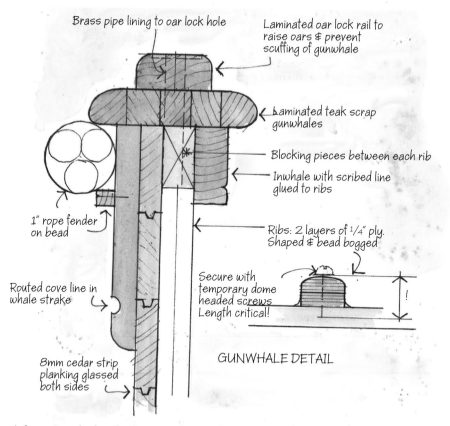

Brass pipe lining to oar lock hole

Laminated oar lock rail to raise oars & prevent scuffing of gunwhale

Laminated teak scrap gunwhales

Blocking pieces between each rib

Inwhale with scribed line glued to ribs

1" rope fender on bead

Ribs: 2 layers of 1/4" ply. Shaped & bead bogged

Routed cove line in whale strake

Secure with temporary dome headed screws Length critical!

8mm cedar strip planking glassed both sides

GUNWHALE DETAIL

a plastic boat. I made the ribs from two layers of 6 mm ply, making a jig so that I could cut the sheets into 20 mm strips across the grain using my son's circular saw. The outer laminations of each rib were shaped like the real thing and the two strips were epoxied together to the inside of the glassed hull with temporary fixing screws. Luckily, the original mould lines were still visible so I fitted ribs over these first and installed two more ribs between them. It takes a bit of work to get these looking right because they may be at 8′ at the keel, but this increases as you get up towards the gunwale. All you can do is to mark equal spaces between the ribs and use your eye to get them to look right.

I initially tried to steam lengths of 2 x ½ inch hardwood along their wider axis for gunwale capping...don't even think about it. A week of evenings wasted to find out that timber doesn't want to bend this way. Then I found a source of teak scraps from a furniture manufacturer who kindly sawed them into 15 mm square profiles, more or less, which I could laminate, in situ, as you can see in the section. The smart routed cove line in the sheer strake was made by a volunteer at the Wooden Boat Show who generously offered to come round to demonstrate his prowess with a router. He also brought 23 friends from the local Wood Work Society; each one showed me how just about everything I had done so far could have been done quicker and more efficiently, and ate us out of fruit cake. They even made me a little jig with a screw head projecting from a hardwood block I could scribe in those little grooves real boats have in their inwhales and risings. So simple...

11. Teak

It's lovely stuff and I was lucky enough to be given a few planks in Indonesia as a gift from a contractor that I herniad back to Oz as hand baggage. There was enough to make the seats and

– joy of joys – a teak transom. However, the 1,500mm long planks were 200 x 20mm and I would need to join three of them together for the transom, making as neat a job as I could. You can get a special tool for centring dowels in jointing timbers, but I did not have one so I cut up length of fluted dowel into about 40 bits. (They need to be fluted so that the glue can penetrate the sides.) I popped them into the appropriate holes drilled into face A, a touch of coloured chalk on the end of the dowels gave me the location of the dowel on the mating face B.

To allow for pilot error, I made the biggest hole I could here, without weakening the transom. I gave it a trial fit and then epoxied everything in sight and clamped it all together as shown in the sketch. When you have sanded your glued up transom to death, just take the long blade out of a craft knife and use it as a scraper. Before your very eyes, the grain will come beautifully alive in the way that sandpaper can never do.

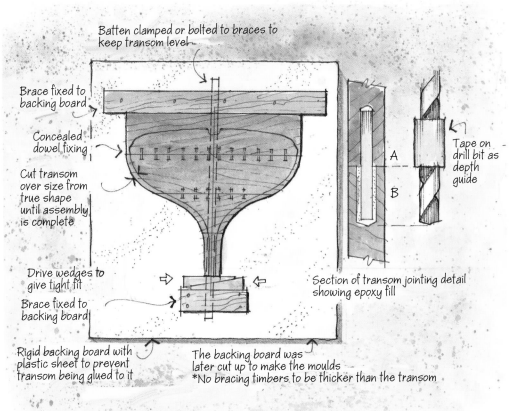

Batten clamped or bolted to braces to keep transom level

Brace fixed to backing board

Concealed dowel fixing

Cut transom over size from true shape until assembly is complete

Drive wedges to give tight fit

Brace fixed to backing board

Rigid backing board with plastic sheet to prevent transom being glued to it

A
B

Tape on drill bit as depth guide

Section of transom jointing detail showing epoxy fill

The backing board was later cut up to make the moulds
*No bracing timbers to be thicker than the transom

BUILDING THE TRANSOM

12. Sandpaper
While we are on the subject, don't waste your time on trying to smooth epoxy with the regular sandpaper; get the industrial strength stuff that car body repair shops use, particularly on torture boards (see 'Bead Bogging Works'). For all other uses, use a sanding block. I used bits of old packing case polystyrene, and gloves. Otherwise, however carefully you are in folding abrasive paper, you can lose your fingerprints in a weekend.

13. Bead Bogging Works

I was shown this technique by Ian Smith, a well known Sydney boat builder. Take a scrap of any old ply, about a foot by 18 inches, cut a series of small 'V's about ⅛ foot at 2 foot centres like this.

After you have glassed your hull and sanded off the imper-fections, you use this plywood panel to apply ridges of thickened epoxy from keel to gunwale, the length of the hull. Then, make up your torture board from ply about three feet by six inches and rig up a way of clamping 80 grade grit paper to it. I used large paper spring clips. You also need some handles so you can get a good grip. Torture board along the length of the hull, when the epoxy

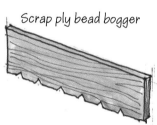

Scrap ply bead bogger

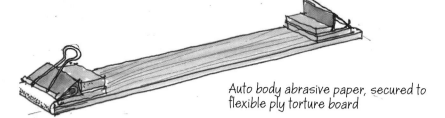

Auto body abrasive paper, secured to flexible ply torture board

has set. I took my watch off and torture boarded one side from early morning until dark. The next day, I did the other side. It is so boring, you don't need your watch to remind you how long all this is taking. Here's an exaggerated sketch of what happens. If there is a hollow, as the board removes the ridges and fairs the hull, the ridges will remain. This allows you to trowel on more epoxy mix to the level of the top of the ridges. Keep going with the board and all will be well.

I don't know if it is called a torture board because of what it does to the hull surface or your lower back at the end of the day... You use progressively finer paper, and then I wound up with wet and dry on sheets of polystyrene foam. Then you can spray the surface gloss black and get the sort of finish that is more suited to a Bentley's bonnet than a rowing boat on Patonga Creek. Not only did I have a flawless finish but I had to drill a new hole to take a reef in my belt. Honest.

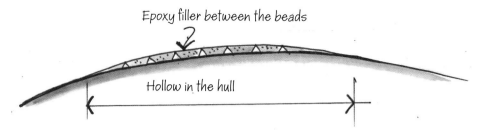

Epoxy filler between the beads

Hollow in the hull

14. The mast

Bruce, my timber supplier, recommended a hollow bird's mouth mast. No, I did not know what he was talking about either. I gave him the mast dimensions and he brought eight 16 foot lengths of tapered, notched, clear grain Oregon from Queensland to his stand at the Sydney Wooden Boat Show. We also dragged the smoothed but unfinished hull from under the house and exhibited her as a project under construction using excellent all-Aussie products. Just like a TV chef, we glued up the mast before our live audience in ten minutes... 'Now, we got this really wicked bit of fresh Oregon which Bruce prepared earlier... Easy peasey...'

Bruce worked out the taper for the mast the old fashioned way; he gave the problem to his computer. Without his help, I would have drawn regular sections of the mast to scale and measured them to get the taper. The mast stiffened up considerably over the next few days and took very little smoothing with a number 5 plane. Just remember to pad your sawhorses with carpet offcuts to avoid bruising this soft timber. In my haste to get afloat, I rushed the gaff and boom – and it shows. In the future, I would make all the fiddly bits first and finish with the hull.

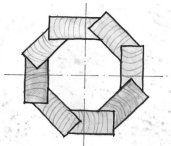

The bird's mouth mast section

15. Oars

I enjoyed making these. They were originally a pair of eight foot oars which I made for my boy's Mirror dinghy so that they could learn to row it instead of prying it along with its original equipment. With her five foot beam, the *Queen* would need at least ten foot oars; I decided to extend them to 10 foot 6 inches on the basis that you can always cut a bit off but you can't cut a bit on. The sketch shows how this was done. I left the ends square, just like the old timers did. After experiencing the advantages of square ended oars, I can see no justification for round ones, unless it suites somebody's industrial mass production process. Firstly, the oars are so much better balanced, you can row for hours without fatigue and they are so much better behaved in the boat. Less rolling around. I finished mine with hardwood tips and some epoxy soaked nylon cord to limit abrasion...

I dismembered an old leather briefcase for the leathers only to find this 'on special' bargain was, in fact, real plastic. A frantic call to a local leather supplier the day before the launch suggested I had to buy a whole hide. I explained my requirement to a helpful all-Aussie Sheila who came up with the perfect all Aussie answer: stubby holders! A leather kit of parts to wrap around your beer bottle (stubby) or can (tinny) to keep the beer cooler and to avoid calluses for the most enthusiastic beer drinker...

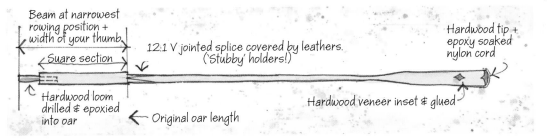

Beam at narrowest rowing position + width of your thumb.
Suare section
12:1 V jointed splice covered by leathers. ('Stubby' holders!)
Hardwood tip + epoxy soaked nylon cord
Hardwood loom drilled & epoxied into oar
Original oar length
Hardwood veneer inset & glued

16. Paint

If you are using contemporary materials to build your classic, it makes sense to keep going with contemporary finishes. I initially brushed on a coat of regular oil-based paint on the topsides for her debut at the Boat Show. Too many brush marks and not enough shine, so I scraped all of this off with the help of a borrowed heat gun, and wet and dried the two-pack water-based polyurethane undercoat to death. A friend kindly offered to spray the water-based black paint with a clear coat on top. We turned the hull sideways, so that the main surfaces were horizontal and we could lay the paint on with gravity working with us, one side at a time. The white paint inside and on the bottom was applied with a low knap pad with satisfactory results, but for dark colours, I believe that spraying is worth the effort.

17. Varnishing

The difference between a professional looking varnish finish and the amateur look seems to be in the use of the correct fillers and stain. Without grain filler, you will find it hard to lose the pore marks on your finished timber. I used tinted filler on mine and a light teak stain to even up some of the colour variations in my collection of teak scraps that made up the gunwale cappings. Too much stain can dull the look of the grain. Then keep building up those coats of varnish, wet and dry between each coat. I lost track after the first eight on the transom.

18. The centre board

The sketch gives the general idea. I found a large stainless steel nut and bolt in the workshop which seemed the perfect size for the centre board pivot. I installed it, well garnished with lots of clear silicone around the holes in the CB case. Wrong decision. When undergoing trials, the A list of Patonga Creek society discovered the *Queen*'s centre board case was incontinent. This was fixed by doing what I should have done originally: following Pete's drawing and installing a hardwood peg, which is a pivot fix through the board and a sealed fix through the sides with two ply discs screwed and siliconed over each end.

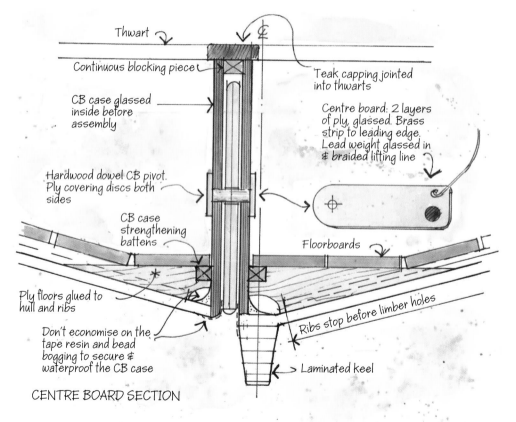

Thwart

Continuous blocking piece

CB case glassed inside before assembly

Teak capping jointed into thwarts

Centre board: 2 layers of ply, glassed. Brass strip to leading edge. Lead weight glassed in & braided lifting line

Hardwood dowel CB pivot. Ply covering discs both sides

CB case strengthening battens

Floorboards

Ply floors glued to hull and ribs

Ribs stop before limber holes

Don't economise on the tape resin and bead bogging to secure & waterproof the CB case

Laminated keel

CENTRE BOARD SECTION

19. Time management

Time wasting on the project was something that will never affect the builder of those plywood clunkers: you cannot help stopping to gaze upon the seductive lines of a true classic as it takes shape before your very eyes. That and looking for the tool you have just put down. The most boring part? Fitting the floors to tie the ribs to the CB case and support and the floorboards... I don't even want to talk about it.

There was nothing difficult in building the *Queen*, just a series of little jobs. It seemed easier to me than building some of the furniture projects I have tacked which demand such straight line accuracy, and was far more satisfying. And you do not waste too much time looking at those as they progress.

20. Launching

A classic boat deserves a classic launch. I made up an invitation for guests and on the spur of the moment, sent one to *Classic Boat* magazine. They printed it and subsequently an edited version of this chapter. The editor suggested I write some more humour pieces. This is not humour, mate, this is true. It all happened.

It was a glorious social event on our little creek, in brilliant sunshine, and the *Queen* was launched by the attractive young widow beneath whose house she had been built. The *Queen* is lucky enough to have her own boat house beneath the widow's holiday home where we built the pontoon. But I am even luckier...

...while undergoing load trials, the 'A' list of Patonga Creek Society discover the *Queen's* centreboard case is incontinent...

EPILOGUE; ALL'S WELL THAT ENDS WELL

I did not tell you earlier that I had been widowed just before my landlady lost her husband or you would have been turning to the back of the book to look for a happy ending. Well, here it is. We were married soon after the launch and the *Queen* was used to ferry guests over the creek to our post-wedding celebrations...

Quirkie's Quotes

A glossary of terms used in the book

Adultery *n.* National sport of colonial Kenya.

Australia *n.* A nation of abstemious introverts with no interest in sport. Do not go there.

Africa *n.* Lost continent.

Alcohol *n.* A much misunderstood vitamin (P G Wodehouse).

Biggles *n.* Fictional British flying hero created by Flying Officer W E Johns who gave himself the fictional title of 'Captain'.

Bertie Wooster *n.* Fictional English twit in the Jeeves stories. Thank you P G Wodehouse.

Bastard *n.* Australian term of endearment.

Birmingham 1. *n.* Black hole right here on planet earth. 2. *n.* A good place to be from.

Black Country *n.* Today they tell you it's because of the wealth of coal beneath the surface. Rubbish: it was the colour of everything from the pollution.

Black Country dialect *n.* Unintelligible. Related as much to Sanskrit as to English.

Col Fawcett *n.* Set off to look for the Lost City of Gold in 1925. Still looking.

ChiBemba *n.* Lingua franca of Zambia.

Dhoti *n.* Indian loin cloth.

Duka *n.* Hindi for shop.

D Cup *n.* A perfect handful.

Dyarchy 1. *n.* Jack Giles' magnificent 46 foot gaff cutter 2. *n.* Government controlled by 2 rulers.

English *n.* National language of India, but not apparently of Birmingham.

Ford Popular 1. *n.* British Trabant. 2. *n.* Lowest form of motoring life. Ever.

Ford's answer to the V.W
0–60 mph 1100cc V.W. = 28.5 secs
0–60 mph Ford Pop. Not in your lifetime.

France *n.* One of the teams at Trafalgar whose National Maritime Museum has never heard of the event.

French *adj.* Please send your entry c/o the publishers...

Goon Show, The *n.* Finest ever radio comedy.

Grandchildren *n.* Delightful packages of perpetual motion.

Hiscocks *n.* World girdlers in lots of Wanderers.

India *n.* Suburb of Birmingham.

Junkers 88 *n.* German bomber. Expired airframe ones were used as guided bombs.

Kuke *n.* colloq. Kikuyu, dominant tribe of Kenya.

Ken Dodd *n.* Dentally challenged comedian.

Kiwi or **New Zealander** *n.* Rugby worshipper with a speech impediment.

Long neck *n.* 26 0z beer bottle.

Melbourne *n.* See Birmingham.

Ken Dodd advertising NHS teeth

Noo Joisey *adj.* Dialect of New Jersey, the Garden State.

Norman Wisdom *n.* Sartorially challenged pratfalling comedian.

Norman Wisdom voted best dressed man of the year by the New Zealand Rag Pickers Gazette 1955.

PC *adj.* Political Correctness. Done more damage to Britain than the Luftwaffe.

Pith Helmet *n.* Ethencial headgear for exthploring the tropicths.

Pimm's *n.* Fuel for above occupation.

Queen of the Creek *n.* See page 82

Riley *n.* Fine leather lined sports saloon.

Seth Efrican *n.* See Kiwi

Swahili *n.* Arabic based lingua franca of East Africa.

Stubby *n.* (plural: shorts) Short beer.

Sheila *n.* Australian female.

Steptoed *vb.* To scrounge or collect junk and rubbish. ETYMOLOGY: from Simpson and Galton's 60s TV sitcom, *Steptoe and Son*, (ripped off by the yanks as *Sanford and Son*).

Sundowner *n.* First beer of the day.

Tinny 1. *n.* Aluminium boat 2. *n.* a can of beer.

Ton Ton Macouts *n.* Haitian secret police thugs. (Haiti has only had independence since 1804; making progress, aren't they?)

VB *n.* Victoria Bitter. Fuels as much of Australia as nuclear energy does France.

Watermelon Necklace *n.* What do you think?

Wolverhampton *n.* Have you ever been there?

Worrah *n.* colloq. US for water.

Wigan pier *n.* Mythical destination. Believed to have been discovered as coal wharf on the canal.

Wolfitt *n.* Sir Donald. Shakespearian actor/manager famous for his eyebrows and interpretation of *King Lear*.

Grandchildren – delightful packages of perpetual motion...